New ACT MATH PRACTICE BOOK

AMERICAN MATH ACADEMY

By H. TONG, M.Ed.

Math Instructional & Olympiad Coach
www.americanmathacademy.com

AMERICAN MATH ACADEMY

NEW ACT MATH PRACTICE BOOK

Writer: H.Tong
Copyright © 2019 The American Math Academy LLC.

All rights reserved. No part of this publication may be reproduced in whole or in part, stored in a retrieval system, or transmitted in any form or by any means electronic, mechanical, photocopying, recording or otherwise, without written permission of the copyright owner.

Printed in United States of America.

ISBN: 9781091552449

ACT is registered trademark of the College Entrance Examination Board, which is not involved in the production of, and does not endorse, this product.

Although the writer has made every effort to ensure the accuracy and completeness of information contained this book, the writer assumes no responsibility for errors, inaccuracies, omissions or any inconsistency herein. Any slighting of people, places, or organizations unintentional.

Questions, suggestions or comments, please email: americanmathacademy@gmail.com

TABLE OF CONTENTS

CHAPTER I PRE-ALGEBRA
Sample ACT Questions —————————————————————————————— 1
Exponents & Radicals Test 1 ———————————————————————— 12
Ratios, Proportions & Variations Test 2 ——————————————— 18
Rates & Percent Test 3 ——————————————————————————— 25
Numbers, Operations, Factors & Multiples Test 4 ——————— 31
Absolute Value & Inequalities Test 5 ———————————————— 37
Mixed Review Test I ————————————————————————————— 43

CHAPTER II HEART OF ALGEBRA
Linear Equations, System of Equations & Lines Test 6 ——— 49
Functions Test 8 —————————————————————————————————— 58
Statistics & Probability Test 9 —————————————————————— 68
Mixed Review Test II ———————————————————————————— 74

CHAPTER III PASSPORT TO ADVANCED MATH
Polynomials Test 10 ———————————————————————————————— 80
Complex Numbers Test 11 ————————————————————————— 86
Exponential Growth, Decay & Data Interpretation Test 12 —— 92
Sequences &Transformations of Functions Test 13 ————— 99
Permutation and Combination Test 14 —————————————— 108
Mixed Review Test III ———————————————————————————— 112

CHAPTER IV GEOMETRY
Angles & Triangles Test 15 ———————————————————————— 118
Area & Perimeter Test 16 ————————————————————————— 125
Circle Test 17 ———————————————————————————————————— 131
Volume Test 18 —————————————————————————————————— 140
Mixed Review Test IV ———————————————————————————— 146

CHAPTER V PRE-CALCULUS
Trigonometry Test 19 ———————————————————————————— 152
Logarithms Test 20 ————————————————————————————— 158
Matrix Test 21 ——————————————————————————————————— 163
Mixed Review Test V ———————————————————————————— 168

About the Author

Mr. Tong teaches at various private and public schools in both New York and New Jersey. In conjunction with his teaching, Mr. Tong developed his own private tutoring company. His company developed a unique way of ensuring their students' success on the math section of the ACT/SAT. His students, over the years, have been able to apply the knowledge and skills they learned during their tutoring sessions in college and beyond. Mr. Tong's academic accolades make him the best candidate to teach ACT/SAT Math. He received his master's degree in Math Education. He has won several national and state championships in various math competitions and has taken his team to victory in the Olympiads. He has trained students for Math Counts, American Math Competition (AMC), Harvard MIT Math Tournament, Princeton Math Contest, and the National Math League, and many other events. His teaching style ensures his students' success—he personally invests energy and time into his students and sees what and what they're struggling with. His dedication towards his students is evident through his students' achievements.

Acknowledgements

I would like to take the time to acknowledge the help and support of my beloved wife, my colleagues, and my students–their feedback on my book was invaluable. Without everyone's help, this book would not be the same. I dedicate this book to my precious daughter Vera, my inspiration to take on this project.

Sample ACT Questions
Pre - Algebra

1. If $\dfrac{x-2}{y-3} = \dfrac{2}{3}$, then find y in terms of x?

   A) $3x$

   B) $2x$

   C) $\dfrac{1}{2}x$

   D) $\dfrac{5}{2}x$

   E) $\dfrac{3}{2}x$

   Solution:
   $\dfrac{x-2}{y-3} = \dfrac{2}{3}$ (cross multiply)

   $2(y - 3) = 3(x - 2)$

   $2y - 6 = 3x - 6$

   $2y = 3x$

   $y = \dfrac{3}{2}x$

   Correct Answer : E

2. Which of following is equivalent to $\left(\dfrac{x+4}{3}\right)^0$, whenever $x \neq -4$?

   A) 0

   B) 1

   C) 2

   D) 3

   E) 4

   Solution:
   Any number to the zero power is always 1.

   Correct Answer : B

3. $\dfrac{x}{\left(\dfrac{3}{5}\right)} = \dfrac{\left(\dfrac{4}{7}\right)}{\left(\dfrac{3}{20}\right)}$ Find x.

   A) $\dfrac{1}{2}$

   B) $\dfrac{2}{7}$

   C) $1\dfrac{1}{2}$

   D) $3\dfrac{1}{7}$

   E) $2\dfrac{2}{7}$

   Solution:
   First find the reciprocal of the fraction then multiply the number by the reciprocal of the fraction.

   $\dfrac{5 \cdot x}{3} = \dfrac{4}{7} \cdot \dfrac{20}{3}$

   $105x = 240$

   $x = \dfrac{240 \div 15}{105 \div 15} = \dfrac{16}{7} = 2\dfrac{2}{7}$

   Correct Answer : E

4. Which of the following is equal to $\dfrac{8^2 \cdot 16^3}{2^{10}}$?

   A) 2^8

   B) 2^7

   C) 2^5

   D) 2^4

   E) 2^2

   Solution:
   $\dfrac{8^2 \cdot 16^3}{2^{10}} = \dfrac{2^6 \cdot 2^{12}}{2^{10}} = \dfrac{2^{18}}{2^{10}} = 2^8$

   Correct Answer : A

Sample ACT Questions
Pre - Algebra

5. The ratio of K(x) to J(x) is $\frac{5}{7}$. If J(x)= 2x–3, what is K(x) in terms of x?

A) 10x – 5

B) 5x – 2

C) $\frac{10x-7}{5}$

D) $\frac{10x-15}{7}$

E) $\frac{7-15}{10}$

Solution:

If ratio of $\frac{K(x)}{J(x)} = \frac{5}{7}$ and J(x) = 2x – 3 then we can find K(x) with proportion.

$\frac{K(x)}{2x-3} = \frac{5}{7}$ (cross multiply)

7 · K(x) = 5 · (2x – 3)

7 · K(x) = 10x – 15

K(x) = $\frac{10x-15}{7}$

Correct Answer : D

6. The students of a school belong to different languages backgrounds. The number of Hindi language students is 350, the number of Spanish language students is 220, and the number of Turkish language students is 130. Find the ratio of Hindi language students to the total number of all language students.

A) 1 to 2

B) 2 to 3

C) 3 to 4

D) 4 to 5

E) 5 to 6

Solution:

The # of Hindi language students is 350 and the total number of languages students are 700. The ratio of Hindu language students to the total number of all language students = $\frac{350}{700} = \frac{1}{2}$ or 1 to 2

Correct Answer : A

Sample ACT Questions
Pre - Algebra

7. There are 'x' math books and 'y' science books on a shelf. The ratio of the number of math books to the total number of books on the shelf is:

A) $\dfrac{x}{y}$

B) $\dfrac{y}{x}$

C) $\dfrac{y+x}{x}$

D) $\dfrac{x}{x+y}$

E) x

Solution:

Number of math books: x

Total number of books: x+y

The ratio of the number of math books to the total number of books: $\dfrac{x}{x+y}$

Correct Answer : D

8. If x is the greatest prime factor of 21 and y is the greatest prime factor of 57, what is the value of x + y?

A) 12

B) 15

C) 26

D) 30

E) 36

Solution:

Use prime factorization to find the greatest prime factor of 21 and 57.

If x is the greatest prime factor of 21, then 21 = 3.7 and the greatest prime factor of 21 is 7. (x = 7)

If y is the greatest prime factor of 57, then 57 = 3.19 and the greatest prime factor of 57 is 19. (y = 19)

x + y = 7 + 19 = 26

Correct Answer : C

3

Sample ACT Questions
Algebra I

9. A school has hired 30 teachers. This is 40% of the number of teachers it expects to have at the end of next academic year. How many teachers does it expect to have next academic year?

A) 25

B) 35

C) 45

D) 75

E) 85

Solution:

Let x equal the total number of teacher in school.

if 30 teachers is 40% of all ⟩ cross multiply
x teachers is 100% of all

$x \cdot 40\% = 30 \cdot 100\%$, then $x = \dfrac{30 \cdot 100}{40} = \dfrac{3000}{40}$

$= 75$ teachers

Correct Answer : D

10. Write the equation in slope – intercept form for the line that passes through the points (–4, 4) and (2, –6).

A) $y = -\dfrac{5}{3}x + \dfrac{10}{3}$

B) $y = \dfrac{5}{3}x + \dfrac{32}{3}$

C) $y = -\dfrac{5}{3}x - \dfrac{32}{3}$

D) $y = -\dfrac{5}{3}x + \dfrac{32}{3}$

E) $y = -\dfrac{5}{3}x + \dfrac{19}{3}$

Solution:

Slope of two points:

$m = \dfrac{y_2 - y_1}{x_2 - x_1}$

$m = \dfrac{-6-(4)}{2-(-4)} = \dfrac{-10}{6} = -\dfrac{5}{3}$

$y = mx + b$ (slope intercept form)

Use (–4, 4) to find b.

$4 = -\dfrac{5}{3}(-4) + b$

$4 = \dfrac{2\cancel{0}}{3\cancel{0}} + b$

$4 - \dfrac{2}{3} = b$

$\dfrac{10}{3} = b$

$y = -\dfrac{5}{3}x + \dfrac{10}{3}$

Correct Answer : A

Sample ACT Questions
Algebra I

11. What is the vertex form of the parabola $y = 3x^2 + 6x - 9$?

A) $f(x) = 3(x + 1)^2 - 12$

B) $f(x) = 3(x + 1)^2 - 6$

C) $f(x) = 3(x - 1)^2 - 4$

D) $f(x) = 3(x - 1)^2 - 9$

E) $f(x) = 3(x - 1)^2 - 12$

Solution:

$y = 3x^2 + 6x - 9$

$y = 3(x^2 + 2x) - 9$

$y = 3(x + 1)^2 - 3 - 9$

$y = 3(x + 1)^2 - 12$

Correct Answer : A

12. A letter is chosen at random from the word "mathematician." What is the probability of choosing either an A or I?

A) $\dfrac{5}{13}$

B) $\dfrac{4}{13}$

C) $\dfrac{13}{5}$

D) 13

D) 18

Solution:

Probability of A or I

total A = 3

total I = 2

$\dfrac{\text{total A and I}}{\text{total letters}} = \dfrac{5}{13}$

Correct Answer : A

Sample ACT Questions
Algebra I

13. If $3y - \dfrac{x}{4} = 10$, then which of the following is equal to $\dfrac{x}{2}$?

A) $6y - 20$

B) $3y - 10$

C) $y - 20$

D) $6y + 20$

E) $y + 20$

Solution:

$$3y - \dfrac{x}{4} = 10$$

$$3y - 10 = \dfrac{x}{4} \longrightarrow \text{multiply both sides by 2.}$$

$$2(3y - 10) = \dfrac{x}{4}(2)$$

$$6y - 20 = \dfrac{x}{2}$$

Correct Answer : A

14. Simplify $\dfrac{x^2 - 8x + 15}{x^2 - 9} \div \dfrac{x^2 - 4x - 5}{x^2 + 3x}$

A) $x - 1$

B) $\dfrac{x}{x + 1}$

C) $x + 1$

D) $\dfrac{x + 1}{x - 1}$

E) $\dfrac{x - 2}{x + 2}$

Solution:

$$\dfrac{x^2 - 8x + 15}{x^2 - 9} \div \dfrac{x^2 - 4x - 5}{x^2 + 3x}$$

$$\dfrac{\cancel{(x-5)}\cancel{(x-3)}}{\cancel{(x-3)}(x+3)} \cdot \dfrac{x\cancel{(x+3)}}{\cancel{(x-5)}(x+1)}$$

$$= \dfrac{x}{x + 1}$$

Correct Answer : B

Sample ACT Questions
Algebra II

15. Solve for x in the equation below:
$$x^2 + 4x + 5 = 0$$

A) $2 \mp i$

B) $-2 \mp i$

C) $2 - i$

D) $2 + i$

E) $2i$

Solution:

$x^2 + 4x + 5 = 0$ (Use the complete square method to solve equation)

$x^2 + 4x = -5$

$(x + 2)^2 - 4 = -5$

$(x + 2)^2 = -5 + 4$

$(x + 2)^2 = -1 \quad i^2 = -1$

$x + 2 = \pm i$

$x = -2 \pm i$

Correct Answer : B

16. In college, next year's tuition will increase by 15% per credit. If this year's tuition in college was $660, what will it be next year?

A) $650

B) $688

C) $745

D) $759

E) $810

Solution:

Increasing tuition $\$660 \cdot \dfrac{15}{100} = \dfrac{9900}{100} = \$99$

Next year tuition total $= \$660 + \$99 = \$759$

Correct Answer : D

17. If $a_n = 2^{n-1}$, then what is the 4th term of this sequence?

A) 4

B) 8

C) 12

D) 15

E) 18

Solution:

Since $a_n = 2^{n-1}$, then 4th term

$a_4 = 2^{4-1}$

$a_4 = 2^3$

$ = 8$

Correct Answer : B

Sample ACT Questions
Algebra II

18. Φ and ⊕ are functions on real numbers.

$x \, \Phi \, y = \dfrac{x^2+y}{4}$ and $x \oplus y = \dfrac{3xy}{5}$

$(2 \, \Phi \, 1) \oplus (3 \, \Phi \, 1) = ?$

A) $\dfrac{25}{4}$

B) $\dfrac{27}{4}$

C) $\dfrac{15}{8}$

D) $\dfrac{17}{2}$

E) $\dfrac{15}{12}$

Solution:

$(2 \, \Phi \, 1) = \dfrac{2^2+1}{4} = \dfrac{5}{4}$

$(3 \, \Phi \, 1) = \dfrac{3^2+1}{4} = \dfrac{10}{4}$

$\left(\dfrac{5}{4} \oplus \dfrac{10}{4}\right) = \dfrac{3 \cdot \frac{5}{4} \cdot \frac{10}{4}}{5}$

$= \dfrac{\frac{150}{16}}{5} = \dfrac{150}{16 \cdot 5} = \dfrac{15\cancel{0}}{8\cancel{0}}$

$= \dfrac{15}{8}$

Correct Answer : C

19. How many distinct permutations of the word "mathematicians" begin and end with the letter "a"?

A) 268

B) 364

C) 476

D) 540

E) 560

Solution:

$\dfrac{14!}{(14-3)! \cdot 3!} = \dfrac{14 \cdot 13 \cdot 12 \cdot 11!}{(11)! \cdot 3!} = \dfrac{14 \cdot 13 \cdot 12}{3 \cdot 2}$

$= \dfrac{14 \cdot 13 \cdot \overset{2}{\cancel{12}}}{\underset{1}{\cancel{6}}}$

$= 14 \cdot 13 \cdot 2 = 364$

Correct Answer : B

Sample ACT Questions
Geometry

20.

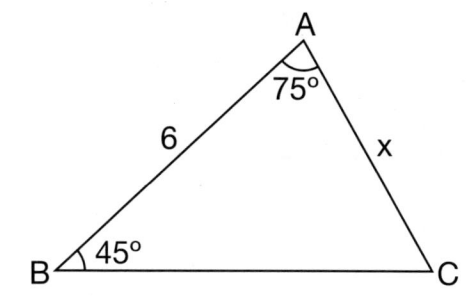

What is the value of x?

A) $\sqrt{6}$

B) $3\sqrt{2}$

C) $2\sqrt{6}$

D) 6

E) 8

Solution:

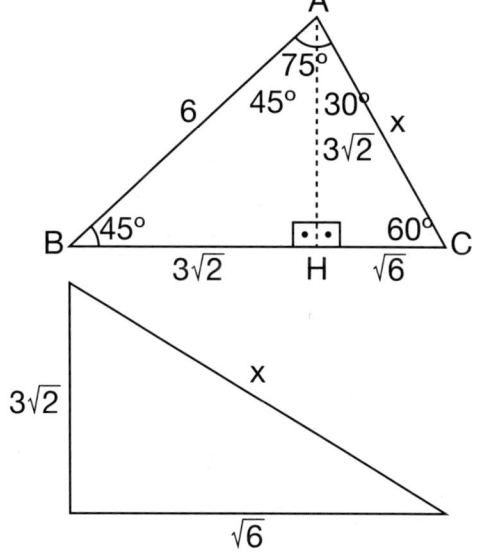

$x^2 = (3\sqrt{2})^2 + (\sqrt{6})^2$

$x^2 = 18 + 6$

$x^2 = 24$

$x = 2\sqrt{6}$

Correct Answer : C

21. Which of the following could not be the third side of a triangle that has sides of lengths 4 and 10?

A) 6

B) 8

C) 9

D) 12

E) 13

Solution:

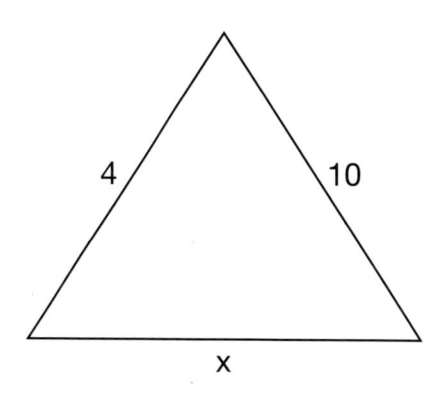

$10 - 4 < x < 10 + 4$

$6 < x < 14$

Correct Answer : A

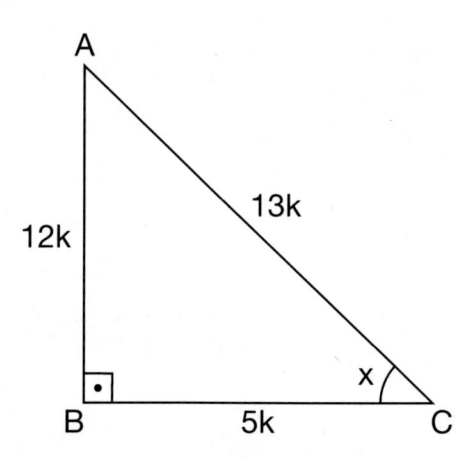

Sample ACT Questions
Pre - Calculus

22. In the following figure P is the center of circle, find the area of the shaded region.

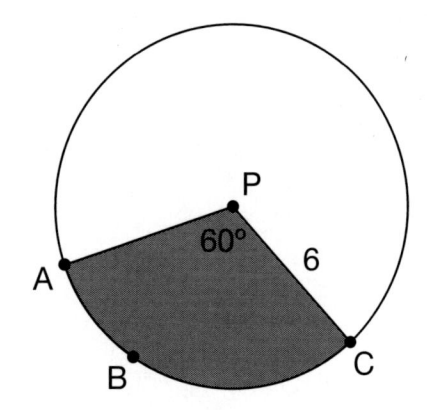

A) 3π

B) 6π

C) 9π

D) 12π

E) 15π

Solution:

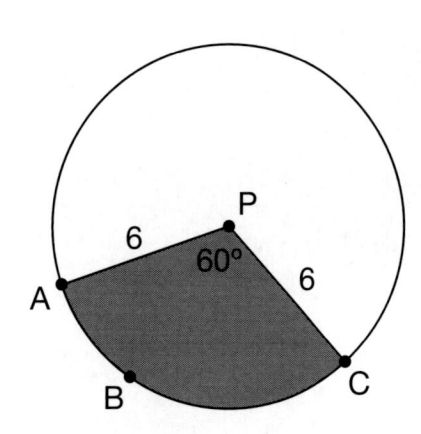

Shaded Area $= \dfrac{\pi r^2 \alpha}{360}$

$= \dfrac{\pi 36 \cdot 6\cancel{0}}{36\cancel{0}}$

$= 6\pi$

Correct Answer : B

23. In a right triangle, one angle measures $x°$, where $\cos x° = \dfrac{5}{13}$.

What is the $\tan(90 - x°)$?

A) $\dfrac{12}{13}$

B) $\dfrac{5}{12}$

C) $\dfrac{7}{12}$

D) $\dfrac{13}{12}$

E) $\dfrac{13}{14}$

Solution:

$\tan(90 - x°) = \cot x° = \dfrac{5\cancel{k}}{12\cancel{k}} = \dfrac{5}{12}$

Correct Answer : B

Sample ACT Questions
Pre - Calculus

24. What is the value of x in the equation
$\log_2(x-2) + \log_2(x+3) = \log_2 6$

A) 1

B) 2

C) 3

D) 4

E) 5

Solution:

$\log_2(x-2) + \log_2(x+3) = \log_2 6$

$\log_2(x-2)(x+3) = \log_2 6$

$(x-2)(x+3) = 6$

$x^2 + x - 6 = 6$

$x^2 + x - 12 = 0$

$(x-3)(x+4) = 0$, then x = 3 or x = −4, since −4 can not be solution x can only be 3.

Correct Answer : C

25. The matrix $Y = \begin{bmatrix} 3 & 6 \\ 4 & 7 \end{bmatrix}$ and, $X - Y = \begin{bmatrix} 1 & 3 \\ 2 & 4 \end{bmatrix}$ then which of following gives matrix X?

A) $\begin{bmatrix} 4 & 9 \\ 6 & 11 \end{bmatrix}$

B) $\begin{bmatrix} 3 & 6 \\ 4 & 7 \end{bmatrix}$

C) $\begin{bmatrix} 1 & 3 \\ 2 & 4 \end{bmatrix}$

D) $\begin{bmatrix} 0 & 1 \\ 2 & 4 \end{bmatrix}$

E) $\begin{bmatrix} 4 & 9 \\ 2 & 4 \end{bmatrix}$

Solution:

$X = Y + \begin{bmatrix} 3 & 6 \\ 4 & 7 \end{bmatrix} \Rightarrow X = \begin{bmatrix} 3 & 6 \\ 4 & 7 \end{bmatrix} + \begin{bmatrix} 1 & 3 \\ 2 & 4 \end{bmatrix} = \begin{bmatrix} 4 & 9 \\ 6 & 11 \end{bmatrix}$

Correct Answer : A

26. If $\cos x + \sin x = \sqrt{5} + 1$, then find $\cos x \cdot \sin x = ?$

A) $\dfrac{5 - 2\sqrt{5}}{2}$

B) $\dfrac{5 + 2\sqrt{5}}{2}$

C) $5 - \sqrt{5}$

D) $2 + \sqrt{5}$

E) $2 - \sqrt{5}$

Solution:

$(\cos x + \sin x)^2 = (\sqrt{5} + 1)^2$

$\rightarrow \cos^2 x + 2\cos x \cdot \sin x + \sin^2 x = 5 + 2\sqrt{5} + 1$

$\rightarrow \cos^2 x + \sin^2 x = 1 \Rightarrow$

$1 + 2\cos x \cdot \sin x = 6 + 2\sqrt{5}$, then

$\sin x \cdot \cos x = \dfrac{5 + 2\sqrt{5}}{2}$

Correct Answer : B

CHAPTER I PRE - ALGEBRA
Exponents & Radicals Test 1

1. $\left(\left(-\frac{2}{3}\right)^4\right)^5$ Is equivalent to:

   A) $\left(\frac{3}{2}\right)^{20}$

   B) $\left(\frac{2}{3}\right)^{20}$

   C) $\left(\frac{4}{3}\right)^{20}$

   D) 3^{20}

   E) 2^{20}

2. Which of following is equivalent to $\left(\frac{x+4}{3}\right)^0$, whenever $x \neq -4$?

   A) 0
   B) 1
   C) 2
   D) 3
   E) 4

3. $(-1)^2 \cdot (-1)^3 \cdot (-1)^{25}$ is equivalent to:

   A) 1
   B) 2
   C) 3
   D) 4
   E) 5

4. $\left.\begin{array}{l}a=3^n\\b=2^n\end{array}\right\}$, then find 18^n in terms of a and b.

   A) $a \cdot b$
   B) $a^2 \cdot b$
   C) $a \cdot b^2$
   D) $a^2 \cdot b^2$
   E) $a^3 \cdot b^{2i}$

5. If $a = 3^b$, then find $3^{(4b+1)}$ in terms of a.

   A) a^2
   B) a^3
   C) a^4
   D) $3a^4$
   E) $3a^3$

6. Which of the following is equal to $\frac{8^2 \cdot 16^3}{2^{10}}$?

   A) 2^8
   B) 2^7
   C) 2^5
   D) 2^4
   E) 2^2

12

Exponents & Radicals Test 1

7. If $x = \dfrac{2^5}{\sqrt{8}}$, then find x.

A) $2\sqrt{2}$

B) $4\sqrt{2}$

C) $6\sqrt{2}$

D) $8\sqrt{2}$

E) $10\sqrt{2}$

8. What is the solution of the equation given below?

$$\dfrac{\sqrt{2} \cdot 6^{\frac{1}{3}}}{\sqrt[3]{3} \cdot 2^{-\frac{1}{6}}}$$

A) 1

B) 2

C) 3

D) 4

E) 5

9. What is the solution of the equation given below?

$$\dfrac{\sqrt{3} \cdot \sqrt[3]{27}}{\sqrt[3]{8} \cdot \sqrt{2}} = ?$$

A) $\dfrac{3\sqrt{2}}{4}$

B) $\dfrac{2\sqrt{2}}{3}$

C) $\sqrt{2}$

D) $\sqrt{3}$

E) $3\sqrt{3}$

10. If $x > 0$ and $x - 3 = \sqrt{x-3}$, then which of the following can be x?

A) 0

B) 1

C) 2

D) 4

E) 5

11. $(81x^8)^{\frac{1}{4}}$

Which of the following equations is equivalent to the expression above?

A) x^2

B) $3x^2$

C) $\dfrac{1}{2}x^2$

D) $5x^2$

E) $9x^2$

12. If $3^x \cdot 3^x \cdot 3^x = 27^4$, then find x.

A) 1

B) 2

C) 3

D) 4

E) 5

Exponents & Radicals Test 1

13. If $a=\sqrt{3}$ and $b=\sqrt{2}$, then find $\dfrac{a}{b}-\dfrac{b}{a}$.

A) $\dfrac{\sqrt{6}}{6}$

B) $\dfrac{1}{\sqrt{5}}$

C) $\dfrac{1}{\sqrt{3}}$

D) $\dfrac{1}{\sqrt{2}}$

E) $6\sqrt{6}$

14. What is the solution(s) for y in the following equation?

$$\dfrac{12}{\sqrt[5]{y}}=6$$

A) 16 and −16

B) 32 and −32

C) 16 only

D) 32 only

E) −16 and 32

15. Simplify $\dfrac{\sqrt{a}}{2-\sqrt{a}}$.

A) $\dfrac{2\sqrt{a}+a}{4-a}$

B) $\dfrac{\sqrt{a}-a}{4-a}$

C) $\dfrac{\sqrt{a}-a}{a}$

D) $\dfrac{2}{4-a}$

E) $\dfrac{2\sqrt{a}-a}{a}$

Exponents & Radicals Test 1
Answer Key

1)	B
2)	B
3)	A
4)	B
5)	D
6)	A
7)	D
8)	B
9)	A
10)	D
11)	B
12)	D
13)	A
14)	D
15)	A

Exponents & Radicals Test 1
Solutions

1. $\left(\left(-\frac{2}{3}\right)^4\right)^5 = \left(-\frac{2}{3}\right)^{4\cdot 5} = \left(-\frac{2}{3}\right)^{20} = \left(\frac{2}{3}\right)^{20}$

Correct Answer : B

2. Any number to the zero power is always 1.

Correct Answer : B

3. $(-1)^2 \cdot (-1)^3 \cdot (-1)^{25} = (1)(-1)(-1) = 1$

Correct Answer : A

4. $18 = 2 \cdot 3^2$
$18^n = (2 \cdot 3^2)^n$
$\quad = 2^n \cdot (3^2)^n$
$\quad = 2^n \cdot (3^n)^2$
$\quad = a^2 \cdot b$

Correct Answer : B

5. $3^{4b+1} = 3^{4b} \cdot 3^1$
$\quad = (3^b)^4 \cdot 3^1$
$\quad = 3a^4$

Correct Answer : D

6. $\dfrac{8^2 \cdot 16^3}{2^{10}} = \dfrac{2^6 \cdot 2^{12}}{2^{10}} = \dfrac{2^{18}}{2^{10}} = 2^8$

Correct Answer : A

7. $x = \dfrac{2^5}{\sqrt{8}}$

$x = \dfrac{32}{2\sqrt{2}}$ (simplify)

$x = \dfrac{16}{\sqrt{2}}$ (multiply by $\sqrt{2}$ part and whole)

$x = \dfrac{16}{\sqrt{2}} \cdot \dfrac{\sqrt{2}}{\sqrt{2}}$

$x = \dfrac{16\sqrt{2}}{2}$

$x = 8\sqrt{2}$

Correct Answer : D

8. $6^{1/3} = 2^{1/3} \cdot 3^{1/3}$, then

$\dfrac{2^{1/2} \cdot 2^{1/3} \cdot 3^{1/3}}{3^{1/3} \cdot 2^{-1/6}} = 2^{5/6} \cdot 2^{1/6} = 2$

Correct Answer : B

16

Exponents & Radicals Test 1
Solutions

9. $\dfrac{\sqrt{3}\cdot\sqrt[3]{27}}{\sqrt[3]{8}\cdot\sqrt{2}} = \dfrac{\sqrt{3}\cdot\sqrt[3]{3^3}}{\sqrt[3]{2^3}\cdot\sqrt{2}} = \dfrac{\sqrt{3}\cdot 3}{2\sqrt{2}} = \dfrac{3}{2\sqrt{2}}$

$= \dfrac{3\cdot(\sqrt{2})}{2\sqrt{2}\cdot(\sqrt{2})} = \dfrac{3\sqrt{2}}{4}$

Correct Answer : A

10. $x - 3 = \sqrt{x-3}$

$(x-3)^2 = x - 3$

$x^2 - 6x + 9 = x - 3$

$x^2 - 7x + 12 = 0$

$(x-3)\cdot(x-4) = 0$

$x = 3$ or $x = 4$

Correct Answer : D

11. $(81x^8)^{\frac{1}{4}} = (3^4 x^8)^{\frac{1}{4}} = 3x^2$

Correct Answer : B

12. If $3^x \cdot 3^x \cdot 3^x = 27^4$, then

$3^{x+x+x} = (3)^{3\cdot 4}$

$3^{3x} = 3^{12}$, then $3x = 12$ and $x = 4$

Correct Answer : D

13. $a = \sqrt{3}$ and $b = \sqrt{2}$, then find

$\dfrac{a}{b} - \dfrac{b}{a} = \dfrac{\sqrt{3}}{\sqrt{2}} - \dfrac{\sqrt{2}}{\sqrt{3}} = \dfrac{\sqrt{3}(\sqrt{3})}{\sqrt{2}(\sqrt{3})} - \dfrac{\sqrt{2}(\sqrt{2})}{\sqrt{3}(\sqrt{2})}$

$= \dfrac{\sqrt{9}}{\sqrt{6}} - \dfrac{\sqrt{4}}{\sqrt{6}} = \dfrac{3}{\sqrt{6}} - \dfrac{2}{\sqrt{6}} = \dfrac{1}{\sqrt{6}} = \dfrac{\sqrt{6}}{6}$

Correct Answer : A

14. $\dfrac{12}{\sqrt[5]{y}} = 6$

$\sqrt[5]{y} = \dfrac{12}{6}$

$\sqrt[5]{y} = 2$

$y = 32$

Correct Answer : D

15. $\dfrac{\sqrt{a}}{2-\sqrt{a}} = \dfrac{\sqrt{a}\cdot(2+\sqrt{a})}{(2-\sqrt{a})(2+\sqrt{a})} = \dfrac{2\sqrt{a}+a}{4-a}$

Correct Answer : A

17

Ratios, Proportions & Variations Test 2

1. If $\frac{x-3}{y-4} = \frac{5}{7}$, then find y in terms of x?

A) $7x$

B) $7x - 1$

C) $5x - 1$

D) $\frac{5x-1}{7}$

E) $\frac{7x-1}{5}$

2. Find the missing number in a proportion.

$$\frac{x}{3} = \frac{21}{14}$$

A) $\frac{1}{2}$

B) $1\frac{1}{2}$

C) $2\frac{1}{2}$

D) $3\frac{1}{2}$

E) $4\frac{1}{2}$

3. Which of the following ratio represents the relationship of hours to minutes?

A) 1 to 36

B) 1 to 48

C) 1 to 60

D) 60 to 1

E) 1 to 72

4. The ratio of K(x) to J(x) is $\frac{5}{7}$. If J(x) = 2x − 3, what is K(x) in terms of x?

A) $10x - 5$

B) $5x - 2$

C) $\frac{10x-7}{5}$

D) $\frac{10x-15}{7}$

E) $\frac{7-15}{10}$

5. The value of a varies inversely with b and directly with c. The constant of variation is $\frac{2}{5}$. What is the value of b when a = 3 and c = 8?

A) 3

B) 5

C) $\frac{7}{8}$

D) $1\frac{1}{15}$

E) $\frac{1}{15}$

Ratios, Proportions & Variations Test 2

6. Find the ratio of the shaded portion to the unshaded portion in the following figure.

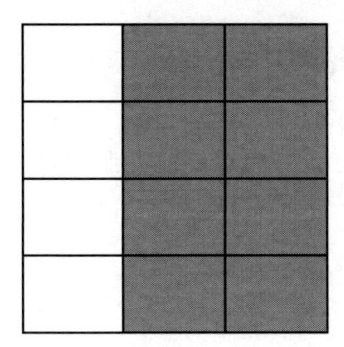

A) $\dfrac{2}{3}$

B) $\dfrac{3}{2}$

C) $\dfrac{4}{5}$

D) 1

E) 2

7. There are 'x' math books and 'y' science books on a shelf. The ratio of the number of math books to the total number of books on the shelf is:

A) $\dfrac{x}{y}$

B) $\dfrac{y}{x}$

C) $\dfrac{y+x}{x}$

D) $\dfrac{x}{x+y}$

E) x

8. In a school, the ratio of the number of student in science class to number of students in math class is 4:9. If the number of students in math class is 27, then find the number of students in science class.

A) 6

B) 9

C) 12

D) 15

E) 18

9. The students of a school belong to different languages backgrounds. The number of Hindi language students is 350, the number of Spanish language students is 220, and the number of Turkish language students is 130. Find the ratio of Hindi language students to the total number of all language students.

A) 1 to 2

B) 2 to 3

C) 3 to 4

D) 4 to 5

E) 5 to 6

Ratios, Proportions & Variations Test 2

10. Melissa answered 27 questions out of 72 questions correctly on her test. Find the ratio of incorrect questions to total questions in simplest form.

A) 2 to 3

B) 5 to 8

C) 8 to 5

D) 3 to 7

E) 7 to 3

11. Two numbers have a ratio of 5 to 7. The larger number is 20 more than $\frac{3}{5}$ of the smaller number. Find the larger number?

A) 15

B) 20

C) 25

D) 30

E) 35

12. Solve the proportion x : 14 = 3 : 7 for x.

A) 3

B) 5

C) 6

D) 8

E) 9

13. The interior angles of a triangle ratio are 4:3:2. How smaller is the smaller angle?

A) 10°

B) 20°

C) 30°

D) 40°

E) 50°

14. If y varies inversely as x and x = 6 when y = 48, find y when x = 8.

A) 6

B) 12

C) 18

D) 24

E) 36

15. Two numbers have a ratio of 5 to 3. If they are positive and differ by 42, what is the value of the smaller number?

A) 63

B) 72

C) 84

D) 92

E) 96

Ratios, Proportions & Variations Test 2
Answer Key

1)	E
2)	E
3)	C
4)	D
5)	D
6)	E
7)	D
8)	C
9)	A
10)	B
11)	E
12)	C
13)	D
14)	E
15)	A

Ratios, Proportions & Variations Test 2
Solutions

1. $\frac{x-3}{y-4} = \frac{5}{7}$ (cross multiply)

$7(x - 3) = 5(y - 4)$

$7x - 21 = 5y - 20$

$7x - 1 = 5y$

$\frac{7x-1}{5} = y$

Correct Answer : E

2. Solution: $\frac{x}{3} = \frac{21}{14}$ (cross multiply)

$14x = 3 \cdot 21$

$14x = 63$

$x = \frac{63}{14}$

$x = \frac{63 \div 7}{14 \div 7} = \frac{9}{2}$

$x = 4\frac{1}{2}$

Correct Answer : E

3. 1 hour = 60 minutes.

Ratio of minutes to hours = 1 to 60

Correct Answer : C

4. If ratio of $\frac{k(x)}{j(x)} = \frac{5}{7}$ and $J(x) = 2x - 3$ then we can find K(x) with proportion.

$\frac{k(x)}{2x-3} = \frac{5}{7}$ (cross multiply)

$7 \cdot K(x) = 5 \cdot (2x - 3)$

$7 \cdot K(x) = 10x - 15$

$K(x) = \frac{10x-15}{7}$

Correct Answer : D

5. $a = k \cdot \frac{c}{b}$

$3 = \frac{2}{5} \cdot \frac{8}{b}$

$3 = \frac{16}{5b}$ (cross multiply)

$15b = 16$

$b = \frac{16}{15} = 1\frac{1}{15}$

Correct Answer : D

6. From figure Shaded portion: 8 and unshaded portion: 4

Ratio from shaded to unshaded is $\frac{8}{4} = 2$

Correct Answer : E

22

Ratios, Proportions & Variations Test 2
Solutions

7. Number of math books: x

Total number of books: x + y

The ratio of the number of math books to the total number of books: $\frac{x}{x+y}$

Correct Answer : D

8. Ratio of students in science class to math class is 4 : 9.

If the number of students in math class is 27, then 9x = 27 and x = 3

Number of students in science class is 4x = 4 · 3 = 12

Correct Answer : C

9. The # of Hindu language students is 350 and the total number of languages students are 700.

The ratio of Hindu language students to the total number of all language students = $\frac{350}{700} = \frac{1}{2}$ or 1 to 2.

Correct Answer : A

10. Incorrect answer 72 – 27 = 45

Ratio of incorrect to total 45 to 72. In simplest form are 5 to 8.

Correct Answer : B

11. Let 5x = smaller number,

7x = larger number

$7x = \frac{3}{5}(5x) + 20$

7x = 3x + 20

7x – 3x = 20

4x = 20

x = 5

Larger number = 7x = 7 · 5 = 35

Correct Answer : E

12. $\frac{x}{14} = \frac{3}{7}$ (cross multiply)

7x = 3 · 14

7x = 42

x = 6

Correct Answer : C

13. Since the interior of triangle angles are always 180^0

The ratio of interior of triangle angles are need to be 180^0

$4x + 3x + 2x = 180^0$.

$9x = 180^0$.

$x = 20^0$.

Smallest angle = $2x = 2 · 20^0 = 40^0$.

Correct Answer : D

Ratios, Proportions & Variations Test 2
Solutions

14. $y = \dfrac{k}{x}$ (Inverse variation)

$k = x \cdot y$, then $k = 6 \cdot 48$, $k = 288$.

When $x = 8$, then $yx = k$

$y \cdot 8 = 288$

$y = 36$

Correct Answer : E

15. If two numbers have a ratio of 5 to 3 and they are positive integers, those numbers can be 5x and 3x.

$5x - 3x = 42$

$2x = 42$

$x = 21$.

Smaller number $= 3x = 3 \cdot 21 = 63$

Value of smaller number is 63.

Correct Answer : A

Rates & Percent Test 3

1. In a class of 20 students, 45% received B's and 30% received A's and the rest of class received C's on a science test. How many students received C?

   A) 3
   B) 5
   C) 6
   D) 8
   E) 9

2. Find the percent for shaded part of the figure below.

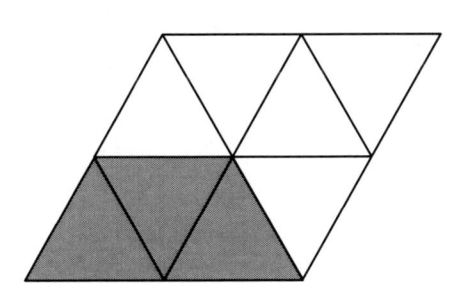

   A) 15%
   B) 22.5%
   C) 32.5%
   D) 37.5%
   E) 44.3%

3. What number is 40% of 30?

   A) 3
   B) 6
   C) 9
   D) 12
   E) 15

4. Write 0.012 as a percent.

   A) 0.12%
   B) 1.2%
   C) 12%
   D) 120%
   E) 1200%

5. A school has hired 30 teachers. This is 40% of the number of teachers it expects to have at the end of next academic year. How many teachers does it expect to have next academic year?

   A) 25
   B) 35
   C) 45
   D) 75
   E) 85

Rates & Percent Test 3

6. On an SAT Math test, Melissa answered 40% of the questions incorrectly. The test contained a total of 55 questions. How many questions did Melissa answer correctly in her SAT math test?

A) 22

B) 33

C) 36

D) 42

E) 48

7. If $\dfrac{x}{\left(\frac{3}{5}\right)} = \dfrac{\left(\frac{4}{7}\right)}{\left(\frac{3}{20}\right)}$ Find x.

A) $\dfrac{1}{2}$

B) $\dfrac{2}{7}$

C) $1\dfrac{1}{2}$

D) $3\dfrac{1}{7}$

E) $2\dfrac{2}{7}$

8. There are 40 students in a class. 28 of those students are boys. What percent of the class are girls?

A) 10%

B) 20%

C) 30%

D) 40%

E) 50%

9. Jessica earned a grade of 85% on her science test that had 40 questions. How many questions on her test did she answer incorrectly?

A) 2

B) 3

C) 4

D) 5

E) 6

10. The school basketball team played 55 games and lost 11 of them. What percent of the games did they win?

A) 30%

B) 40%

C) 60%

D) 80%

E) 90%

Rates & Percent Test 3

11. Jenny paid $96.00 for a shoe that was discounted by 20%. What was the original price of the shoes?

A) $96.00

B) $105.00

C) $112.20

D) $120.00

E) $122.20

12. John took 16 hours to read 320 pages of book. At this rate, how long will it take him to read 600 pages of book?

A) 15

B) 20

C) 25

D) 30

E) 35

13. There are 25 students on the robotics team. If 40% of the team members are boys, How many students on the robotics team are girls?

A) 10

B) 15

C) 20

D) 25

E) 30

14. The population of a city decreased from 360 thousand to 270 thousand in 2018 to 2019. Find the percent of decrease.

A) 5%

B) 10%

C) 15%

D) 20%

E) 25%

15. Vera purchases a combined total of 20 red and pink pens for $90. The red pens cost $4 each and pink pens cost $5 each. How many red pens did Vera purchase?

A) 5

B) 8

C) 10

D) 12

E) 15

Rates & Percent Test 3
Answer Key

1)	B
2)	D
3)	D
4)	B
5)	D
6)	B
7)	E
8)	C
9)	E
10)	D
11)	D
12)	D
13)	B
14)	E
15)	C

Rates & Percent Test 3
Solutions

1. Total students: 20

Students received A: $45\% = \dfrac{45 \cdot 20}{100} = 9$ students

Students received B: $30\% = \dfrac{30 \cdot 20}{100} = 6$ students

Students received C = Total students − (Students received A + Students received B)

Students received C = 20 − (9+6)

Students received C = 20 − 15

Students received C = 5

Correct Answer : B

2. Shaded part: 3

Total: 8

Percent for shaded part =

$\dfrac{3}{8} = \dfrac{3 \cdot (12 \cdot 5)}{8 \cdot (12 \cdot 5)} = \dfrac{37 \cdot 5}{100} = 37.5\%$

Correct Answer : D

3. $\dfrac{40 \cdot 30}{100} = \dfrac{1200}{100} = 12$

Correct Answer : D

4. $0.012 = \dfrac{12}{1000} = 1.2\%$

Correct Answer : B

5. Let x is the total number of teacher in school.

$\left.\begin{array}{l}\text{if 30 teachers is 40\% of all}\\ \text{x teachers is 100\% of all}\end{array}\right\}$ cross multiply

$x \cdot 40\% = 30 \cdot 100\%$

then $x = \dfrac{30 \cdot 100}{40} = \dfrac{3000}{40} = 75$ teachers

Correct Answer : D

6. Let x is the total number of correct questions.

If 40% of the questions are incorrectly answered than 60% of questions are correctly answered.

$x = \dfrac{60 \cdot 55}{100} = \dfrac{3300}{100} = 33$ correct answer.

Correct Answer : B

7. First find the reciprocal of the fraction then multiply the number by the reciprocal of the fraction.

$\dfrac{5 \cdot x}{3} = \dfrac{4}{7} \cdot \dfrac{20}{3}$

$\dfrac{5x}{3} = \dfrac{80}{21}$ (Cross multiply)

$5x \cdot 21 = 3 \cdot 80$

$105x = 240$

$x = \dfrac{240 \div 15}{105 \div 15} = \dfrac{16}{7} = 2\dfrac{2}{7}$

Correct Answer : E

8. Total # of students = 40

# of boys = 28

# of girls = 40 − 28 = 12

Percent of girls: $\dfrac{12 \div 4}{40 \div 4} = \dfrac{3 \cdot 10}{10 \cdot 10} = \dfrac{30}{100} = 30\%$

Correct Answer : C

Rates & Percent Test 3
Solutions

9. let x is number of correct questions.

$x = \dfrac{85 \cdot 40}{100} = 34$ correct questions.

Incorrect questions = total questions – correct questions

Incorrect questions = 40 – 34 = 6 incorrect questions

Correct Answer : E

10. let x is the number of game the team won.

x = 55 – 11 = 44 games won.

Percent of game won:

$\dfrac{44}{55} = \dfrac{44 \div 11}{55 \div 11} = \dfrac{4}{5} = \dfrac{4 \cdot 20}{5 \cdot 20} = \dfrac{80}{100} = \%80$

Correct Answer : D

11. let x is the discount price.

Original Price = 100x

after dicount price : 80x

80x = 96

$x = \dfrac{96}{80}$ orijinal price : $100x \dfrac{96}{80} = 120$

Correct Answer : D

12. If in 16 hours read 320 pages of book

In x hours read 600 pages of book

320 · x = 16 · 600

x = 30 hours.

Correct Answer : D

13. Out of 25 students, if 40% are boys

# of boys = $\dfrac{40 \cdot 25}{100} = 10$

# of girls will be 15.

Correct Answer : B

14. Since the population of a City decreased from 360 thousand to 270 thousand

Percent of decrease:

$\dfrac{360 - 270}{360} = \dfrac{90}{360} = \dfrac{1}{4} = 25\%$

Correct Answer : E

15. Total: 20

Of pink: x

Of red: 20 – x

4($20 – x) + 5x = $90

$80 – 4x + 5x = $90

x = $90 – $80

x = $10

Of red: 20 – x = $20 – $10 = $10

Correct Answer : C

Numbers, Operations, Factors & Multiples Test 4

1. Simplify $\left(\dfrac{a}{b}\right)\cdot\left(\dfrac{ab}{cd}\right)\cdot\left(\dfrac{cd}{a^2}\right)$?

   A) a^2

   B) $a^2 \cdot b$

   C) $a \cdot b \cdot c \cdot d$

   D) $a^2 \cdot b \cdot c \cdot d$

   E) 1

2. What is the least common multiple of 4 and 9?

   A) 4

   B) 9

   C) 36

   D) 72

   E) 108

3. Which of following is a prime number?

   A) 2

   B) 4

   C) 9

   D) 10

   E) 12

4. Mr. Tony gave the following list of numbers to his class. He asked the class to find all of the composite numbers in the list.

   2, 5, 9, 11, 14, 15, 19, 21

   Which of these shows all of the composite numbers in the list?

   A) 2, 5, 11, 19

   B) 14, 15, 21

   C) 2, 5, 14, 11, 19

   D) 2, 5, 11, 15, 19, 21

   E) 2, 5, 9, 11, 14, 15, 19, 21

5. Which of following numbers is the smallest positive integer that when divided by 4 and 7 leave a remainder of 3?

   A) 88

   B) 84

   C) 58

   D) 31

   E) 16

6. If x is a positive number and, $x^2 + x - 12 = 0$, what is the value of x?

   A) 2

   B) 3

   C) 4

   D) 6

   E) 12

Numbers, Operations, Factors & Multiples Test 4

7. If x is the greatest prime factor of 21 and y is the greatest prime factor of 57, what is the value of x + y?

A) 12

B) 15

C) 26

D) 30

E) 36

8. If a, b, c are positive numbers and a · b = 12, b · c = 3, and a · c = 9, then find a · b · c

A) 6

B) 9

C) 12

D) 18

E) 24

9. If $x^{\frac{1}{4}} = 2$ and x · y = 64, then what is the value of y?

A) 1

B) 2

C) 3

D) 4

E) 8

10. Which of following numbers are divisible by 3, 4, and 7?

A) 27

B) 36

C) 42

D) 68

E) 84

11. What is the least common multiple of 7 and 8?

A) 14

B) 21

C) 28

D) 56

E) 84

12. Solve $\dfrac{\frac{1}{3}}{\frac{4}{7}}$?

A) $\dfrac{1}{2}$

B) $\dfrac{3}{7}$

C) $\dfrac{4}{7}$

D) $\dfrac{7}{12}$

E) $\dfrac{4}{12}$

Numbers, Operations, Factors & Multiples Test 4

13. Evaluate $2^3 + (2 + 3) \cdot 4 - 8 + (4+3)^0$.

    A) 18

    B) 21

    C) 24

    D) 28

    E) 34

Numbers, Operations, Factors & Multiples Test 4
Answer Key

1)	E
2)	C
3)	A
4)	B
5)	D
6)	B
7)	C
8)	D
9)	D
10)	E
11)	D
12)	D
13)	B

Numbers, Operations, Factors & Multiples Test 4
Solutions

1. $\left(\dfrac{a}{b}\right) \cdot \left(\dfrac{ab}{cd}\right) \cdot \left(\dfrac{cd}{a^2}\right) = \dfrac{a^2 \cdot b \cdot c \cdot d}{a^2 \cdot b \cdot c \cdot d} = 1$

   Correct Answer : E

2. To find the LCM of 4 and 9, list the multiples.

   Multiples of: 4, 8, 12, 16, 20, 24, and 28, 32, 36

   Multiples of 9: 9, 18, 27, 36

   The lowest multiple that is common to 4 and 9 is 36. So the LCM of 4 and 9 is 36.

   Correct Answer : C

3. Prime numbers: A number that has only two factors, 1 and itself.

   4: Composite number
   9: Composite number
   10: Composite number
   12: Composite number
   2: Prime number

   Correct Answer : A

4. From the list
   Prime number: 2, 5, and 11, 19
   Composite number: 14, 15, 21

   Correct Answer : B

5. From all choices only 31 has a remainder of 3 when divided by 4, and 7 divides.

   Correct Answer : D

6. If x is a positive number and $x^2 + x - 12 = 0$, then $(x - 3)(x + 4) = 0$

   $x - 3 = 0$, or $x + 4 = 0$

   $x = 3$ or $x = -4$

   Correct Answer : B

7. Use prime factorization to find the greatest prime factor of 21 and 57.

   If x is the greatest prime factor of 21, then $21 = 3 \cdot 7$ and the greatest prime factor of 21 is 7. ($x = 7$)

   If y is the greatest prime factor of 57, then $57 = 3 \cdot 19$ and the greatest prime factor of 57 is 19. ($y = 19$)

   $x + y = 7 + 19 = 26$

   Correct Answer : C

8. $a \cdot b = 12$,
   $b \cdot c = 3$,
   $a \cdot c = 9$, then $a^2 \cdot b^2 \cdot c^2 = 12 \cdot 3 \cdot 9$,
   $a^2 \cdot b^2 \cdot c^2 = 324$
   $a \cdot b \cdot c = \sqrt{324}$
   $a \cdot b \cdot c = 18$

   Correct Answer : D

Numbers, Operations, Factors & Multiples Test 4
Solutions

9. If $x^{\frac{1}{4}} = 2$ then $x = 2^4$, $x = 16$

x must be 16

y must be 4

Correct Answer : D

10. A number is divisible by 3 when the sum of the digits is divisible by 3.

A number is divisible by 7, when the last digit of a number is divisible by 7.

A number is divisible by 4, when the last two digits of a number are divisible by 4.

Correct Answer : E

11. To find the LCM of 7 and 8 list the multiples.

Multiples of 7: 7, 14, 21, 28, 35, 42, 47, 56

Multiples of 8: 8, 16, 24, 32, 40, 48, 56

The lowest multiple that is common to 7 and 8 is 56. So the LCM of 7 and 8 is 56

Correct Answer : D

12. $\dfrac{\frac{1}{3}}{\frac{4}{7}}$

keep the first fraction, then change the division sign to multiplication, and then flip the second fraction by switching the top and bottom numbers.

$$\dfrac{\frac{1}{3}}{\frac{4}{7}} = \dfrac{1}{3} \cdot \dfrac{7}{4} = \dfrac{7}{12}$$

Correct Answer : D

13. PEMDAS: Parentheses, Exponents, Multiplication/Division, Addition/Subtraction

$= 2^3 + (2 + 3) \cdot 4 - 8 + (4 + 7)^0$.

$= 8 + (5) \cdot 4 - 8 + 1$

$= 8 + 20 - 8 + 1$

$= 21$

Correct Answer : B

Absolute Value & Inequalities Test 5

1. $$\left|\frac{3x}{4} - 6\right| < 12$$

   What is a possible value of x in the above inequality?

   A) −10
   B) −9
   C) −8
   D) −5
   E) 24

2. For the following inequality which of the following MUST be true?

   $$\frac{2x}{3} - 5 < 9$$

   A) 27
   B) 25
   C) 24
   D) 22
   E) 20

3. $$\frac{4x}{5} - 7 < 9$$

   Which of following is the solution for the inequality?

   A) (∞, 20)
   B) (−∞, 20)
   C) (−∞, 12)
   D) (−∞, −12)
   E) (−20, 20)

4. x and y are integers.

   $$-8 < x < 7$$
   $$1 < y < 11$$

   What is the maximum value of $x^2 + y^2$?

   A) 109
   B) 129
   C) 149
   D) 169
   E) 179

5. If 7x − 12 ≤ 16, then what is the largest possible value of 2x − 1?

   A) 3
   B) 4
   C) 5
   D) 6
   E) 7

6. If 3a + 2b < 48 and a ≥ 6 which of the following statement must be true for b?

   A) b < 15
   B) b > 15
   C) b ≥ 15
   D) b ≤ 15
   E) b = 15

Absolute Value & Inequalities Test 5

7. If $x < 0$, then $\dfrac{|x| + |-2x|}{|-3x|}$ is equal to which of following?

A) –1

B) 0

C) 1

D) 2

E) 5

8. $\dfrac{|-9| + |5|}{|-7|}$ is equal to which of following?

A) 1

B) 2

C) 5

D) 9

E) 12

9. x and y are integers.
$4 < x < 16$ and $\dfrac{x}{y} = \dfrac{5}{7}$, then what is the largest possible value of y?

A) 10

B) 15

C) 18

D) 21

E) 25

10. Evaluate $|-2^2 + (-3)^2|$.

A) –5

B) –1

C) 1

D) 5

E) 13

11. For the following inequality which of the following can be x?

$$|3x - 5| = 2x$$

A) –5

B) –3

C) –1

D) 0

E) 1

12. If x hour is equivalent to y minutes, of the following, which best represents the relationship between x and y?

A) x = y

B) x = 30y

C) x = 60y

D) x = 120y

E) x = 90y

Absolute Value & Inequalities Test 5

13. If $|2x - 7| > 9$, which of following is the graph of the equation?

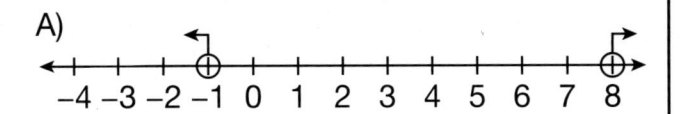

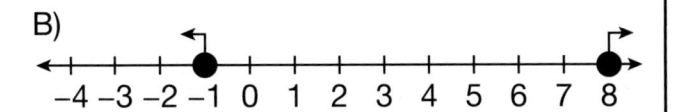

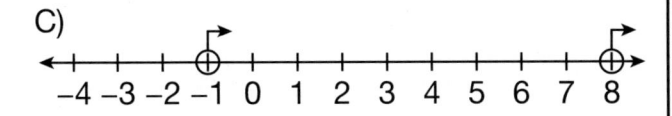

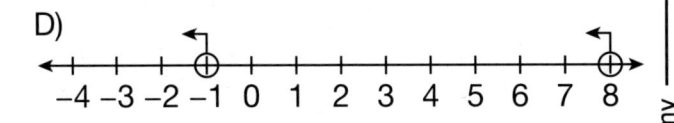

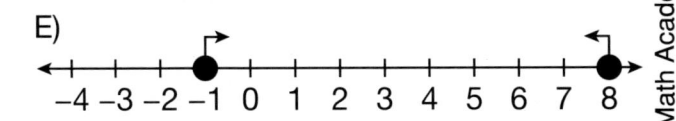

A) number line with open circles at −1 and 8, arrows pointing outward

B) number line with closed circles at −1 and 8, arrows pointing outward

C) number line with open circles at −1 and 8, arrows pointing inward

D) number line with open circles at −1 and 8, arrows pointing inward (reversed)

E) number line with closed circles at −1 and 8, arrows pointing inward

14. Melissa final grade in a math course is 60% of her current grade, plus 30% of her final exam score. If her current grade is 80 and her goal is to get a final grade of 90% or higher score. Which of following is showing correct inequality for this situation?

A) $0.6 \cdot 90 + 0.3 \cdot x \geq 80$

B) $0.6 \cdot 30 + 0.8 \cdot x \geq 90$

C) $0.6 \cdot 80 + 0.3 \cdot x \leq 90$

D) $0.6 \cdot 80 + 0.3 \cdot x \geq 90$

E) $0.6 \cdot 80 + 0.3 \cdot x > 90$

15. Which statement is modeled by $3x + 7 > 10$?

A) The sum of 7 and 3 times x is at most 10.

B) Seven added to the product of 3 and x is greater than 10.

C) Three times x plus 7 is at least 10.

D) The product of 3 and x added to 7 is 10.

E) The product of 7 and x added to 3 is 10.

16. A fitness center has two membership plans. One is a $23 membership fee and $7 per visit and another one is only per visit fees of $13. Which of the following systems of equations can be used to determine the fitness center membership plans?

A) $y = 7 + 23x$
$y = 13$

B) $y = 23 + 7x$
$y = 13x$

C) $y = 13$
$y = 23 + 7x$

D) $y = 13x$
$y = 23x + 7$

E) $y = 23x$
$y = 13x + 7$

Absolute Value & Inequalities Test 5
Answer Key

1)	D
2)	E
3)	B
4)	C
5)	E
6)	A
7)	C
8)	B
9)	D
10)	D
11)	E
12)	C
13)	A
14)	D
15)	B
16)	B

Absolute Value & Inequalities Test 5
Solutions

1. $\frac{3x}{4} - 6 < 12$ or $\frac{3x}{4} - 6 > -12$

   $\frac{3x}{4} < 12 + 6$ or $\frac{3x}{4} > -12 + 6$

   $\frac{3x}{4} < 18$ or $\frac{3x}{4} > -6$

   $3x < 4 \cdot 18$ or $3x > 4(-6)$

   $3x < 72$ or $3x > -24$

   $x < 24$ or $x > -8$

   $-8 < x < 24$

   Correct Answer : D

2. $\frac{2x}{3} - 5 + 5 < 9 + 5$

   $\frac{2x}{3} < 14$

   $2x < 3 \cdot 14$

   $2x < 42$

   $x < 21$

   Correct Answer : E

3. $\frac{4x}{5} - 7 < 9$

   $\frac{4x}{5} - 7 + 7 < 9 + 7$

   $\frac{4x}{5} < 16$

   $4x < 5 \cdot 16$

   $4x < 80$

   $x < 20$, $x = (-\infty, 20)$

   Correct Answer : B

4. Since x and y are integers x can be –7 for max, and y can be 10 for max

   $x^2 + y^2 = (-7)^2 + (10)^2 = 49 + 100 = 149$

   Correct Answer : C

5. If $7x - 12 \leq 16$, $7x - 12 + 12 \leq 16 + 12$,

   $7x \leq 28$

   $x \leq 4$ (multiply both side by 2)

   $2x \leq 8$ (subtract –1 both side)

   $2x - 1 \leq 8 - 1$

   $2x - 1 \leq 7$

   Largest possible value of $2x - 1$ is 7.

   Correct Answer : E

6. Since $3a + 2b < 48$, and $a \geq 6$

   $3 \cdot (6) + 2b < 48$,

   $18 + 2b < 48$,

   $2b < 48 - 18$,

   $2b < 30$

   $b < 15$

   Correct Answer : A

7. Since $x < 0$, then

   $|x| = -x$

   $|-2x| = -2x$

   $|-3x| = -3x$

   So, $\frac{|x| + |-2x|}{|-3x|} = \frac{-x + (-2x)}{-3x} = \frac{-3x}{-3x} = 1$

   Correct Answer : C

Absolute Value & Inequalities Test 5
Solutions

8. $\dfrac{|-9|+|5|}{|-7|} = \dfrac{9+5}{7} = \dfrac{14}{7} = 2$

Correct Answer : B

9. Since x and y are integers and x is between 4 to 16, then x can be maximum 15.

$\dfrac{15}{y} = \dfrac{5}{7}$ (Cross multiply)

$5y = 7 \cdot 15$

$5y = 105$

$y = 21$

Correct Answer : D

10. $|-2^2 + (-3)^2| = |-4 + 9| = |5| = 5$

Correct Answer : D

11. $3x - 5 = 2x$ or $3x - 5 = -2x$.

$3x - 2x = 5$ or $3x + 2x = 5$, $5x = 5$

$x = 5$ or $x = 1$

Correct Answer : E

12. If x hour is equivalent to y minutes:

$x = 60y$

Correct Answer : C

13. The absolute value inequality is equivalent to $|2x - 7| > 9$ or $|2x - 7| < -9$.

	First Inequality		Second Inequality
	$2x - 7 > 9$	Write inequalities.	$2x - 7 < -9$
	$2x > 16$	Add 7 from each side.	$2x < -2$
	$x > 8$	Divide each side by 2.	$x < -1$

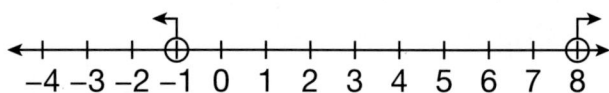

$\leftarrow\!\!+\!\!+\!\!+\!\!\underset{-4\ -3\ -2\ -1}{\oplus}\!\!+\!\!\underset{0\ \ 1\ \ 2\ \ 3\ \ 4\ \ 5\ \ 6\ \ 7}{+\!\!+\!\!+\!\!+\!\!+\!\!+\!\!+\!\!+}\!\!\underset{8}{\oplus}\!\!\rightarrow$

Correct Answer : A

14. Final grade: $0.6 \cdot 80 + 0.3 \cdot x$

$0.6 \cdot 80 + 0.3 \cdot x \geq 90$

Correct Answer : D

15. $3x + 7 > 10 \rightarrow$ Seven added to the product of 3 and x is greater than 10

Correct Answer : B

16. First plan: $23 membership fee and $7 per visit $ convert to the equation.

$y = \$23 + 7x$

Second plan: only per visit fee of $13 $ convert to the equation.

$y = 13x$ (no membership fee)

Correct Answer : B

42

Mixed Review Test I

1. If $a = \sqrt{5}$ and $b = \sqrt{3}$, then find $\frac{a}{b} - \frac{b}{a}$.

   A) $\frac{\sqrt{15}}{15}$

   B) $\frac{2\sqrt{15}}{15}$

   C) $\frac{\sqrt{15}}{5}$

   D) $\frac{4\sqrt{15}}{15}$

   E) $\frac{2\sqrt{15}}{3}$

2. Simplify $\frac{\sqrt{x}}{2+\sqrt{x}}$?

   A) $\frac{2\sqrt{x}-x}{4-x}$

   B) $\frac{\sqrt{x}-x}{4-x}$

   C) $\frac{\sqrt{x}-x}{x}$

   D) $\frac{2}{4-x}$

   E) $\frac{2\sqrt{x}-x}{x}$

3. If $\frac{x-2}{y-3} = \frac{2}{3}$, then find y in terms of x?

   A) $3x$

   B) $5x$

   C) $\frac{1}{2}x$

   D) $\frac{5x}{2}$

   E) $\frac{3}{2}x$

4. The interior angles of a triangle ratio are 8 : 6 : 4. What is the measure of largest angle?

   A) 30°

   B) 40°

   C) 60°

   D) 80°

   E) 90°

5. If y varies inversely as x and x = 10 when y = 18, find y when x = 36.

   A) 1

   B) 3

   C) 5

   D) 7

   E) 9

6. In a class of 20 students, 45% received B's and 30% received A's and rest of class received C's in Science Test. How many students received A?

   A) 3

   B) 5

   C) 6

   D) 8

   E) 9

43

Mixed Review Test I

7. Write 0.015 as a percent.

A) 0.15%

B) 1.5%

C) 15%

D) 150%

E) 1500%

8. If $\dfrac{x}{\left(\frac{2}{5}\right)} = \dfrac{\left(\frac{1}{8}\right)}{\left(\frac{3}{2}\right)}$ Find x.

A) $\dfrac{1}{15}$

B) $\dfrac{1}{30}$

C) $\dfrac{1}{45}$

D) $\dfrac{2}{15}$

E) $\dfrac{1}{20}$

9. The school basketball team played 55 games and lose11 of them. What percent of the games did they lose?

A) 20%

B) 40%

C) 60%

D) 80%

E) 90%

10. If x is a negative number, and $x^2 + x - 12 = 0$, what is the value of x?

A) −2

B) −3

C) −4

D) −6

E) −12

Mixed Review Test I

11. If $\left|\frac{x}{4}-6\right|<7$ what is a possible value of x in the above inequality?

A) −4

B) −10

C) −15

D) 25

E) 52

12. If $3x - 10 \leq 8$, then what is the largest possible value of $3x + 1$?

A) 13

B) 14

C) 15

D) 16

E) 19

13. If $x > 0$, then $\frac{|x|+|-2x|}{|-3x|}$ is equal to which of following.

A) −1

B) 0

C) 1

D) 2

E) 5

14. If x is the greatest prime factor of 26 and y is the greatest prime factor of 55, what is the value of x + y?

A) 8

B) 12

C) 24

D) 30

E) 36

15. The population of a city increased from 270 thousand to 360 thousand in 2017 to 2018. Find the percent of increase.

A) $13.\overline{3}\%$

B) $23.\overline{3}\%$

C) $33.\overline{3}\%$

D) $43.\overline{3}\%$

E) $53.\overline{3}\%$

45

Mixed Review Test I
Answer Key

1)	B
2)	A
3)	E
4)	D
5)	C
6)	C
7)	B
8)	B
9)	A
10)	C
11)	D
12)	E
13)	C
14)	C
15)	C

Mixed Review Test I
Solutions

1. $\dfrac{\sqrt{5}}{\sqrt{3}} - \dfrac{\sqrt{3}}{\sqrt{5}} = \dfrac{\sqrt{5} \cdot \sqrt{5}}{\sqrt{3} \cdot \sqrt{5}} - \dfrac{\sqrt{3} \cdot \sqrt{3}}{\sqrt{5} \cdot \sqrt{3}} = \dfrac{\sqrt{25}}{\sqrt{15}} - \dfrac{\sqrt{9}}{\sqrt{15}}$

$= \dfrac{5}{\sqrt{15}} - \dfrac{3}{\sqrt{15}} = \dfrac{2}{\sqrt{15}} = \dfrac{2 \cdot \sqrt{15}}{\sqrt{15} \cdot \sqrt{15}} = \dfrac{2\sqrt{15}}{15}$

Correct Answer : B

2. $\dfrac{\sqrt{x}}{2+\sqrt{x}} = \dfrac{\sqrt{x} \cdot (2-\sqrt{x})}{(2+\sqrt{x})(2-\sqrt{x})} = \dfrac{2\sqrt{x}-x}{4-x}$

Correct Answer : A

3. $\dfrac{x-2}{y-3} = \dfrac{2}{3}$ (cross multiply)

$2(y-3) = 3(x-2)$

$2y - 6 = 3x - 6$

$2y = 3x$

$y = \dfrac{3}{2}x$

Correct Answer : E

4. Since the interior of triangle angles are always 180°

The ratio of interior of triangle angles are need to be 180°.

$8x + 6x + 4x = 180°$

$18x = 180°$

$x = 10°$

Large angle = $8x = 8 \cdot 10° = 80°$.

Correct Answer : D

5. $y = \dfrac{k}{x}$ (Inverse variation)

$k = x \cdot y$, then $k = 10 \cdot 18$, $k = 180$.

When $x = 36$, then $yx = k$

$y \cdot 36 = 180$

$y = 5$

Correct Answer : C

6. Total students: 20

Students received A: 30% = $\dfrac{30 \cdot 20}{100} = 6$ students

Correct Answer : C

7. $0.015 = \dfrac{15}{1000} = 1.5\%$

Correct Answer : B

8. First find the reciprocal of the fraction then multiply the number by the reciprocal of the fraction.

$\dfrac{5 \cdot x}{2} = \dfrac{1}{8} \cdot \dfrac{2}{3}$

$\dfrac{5x}{2} = \dfrac{2}{24}$ (Cross multiply)

$5x \cdot 24 = 2 \cdot 2$

$120x = 4$

$x = \dfrac{4}{120} = \dfrac{1}{30}$

Correct Answer : B

Mixed Review Test I
Solutions

9. let x is the number of game the team lose.

x = 11 games lose.

Percent of game lose:

$$\frac{11}{55} = \frac{11 \div 11}{55 \div 11} = \frac{1}{5} = \frac{1 \cdot 20}{5 \cdot 20} = \frac{20}{100} = 20\%$$

Correct Answer : A

10. If x is a positive number and

$x^2 + x - 12 = 0$, then $(x - 3)(x + 4) = 0$

$x - 3 = 0$, or $x + 4 = 0$

$x = 3$ or $x = -4$

Correct Answer : C

11. $\frac{x}{4} - 6 < 7$ or $\frac{x}{4} - 6 < -7$

$\frac{x}{4} < 7 + 6$ or $\frac{x}{4} > -7 + 6$

$\frac{x}{4} < 13$ or $\frac{x}{4} > -1$

$x < 4 \cdot 13$ or $x > 4(-1)$

$x < 52$ or $x > -4$

$x < 52$ or $x > -4$

$-4 < x < 52$

Correct Answer : D

12. If $3x - 10 \leq 8$,

$3x - 10 + 10 \leq 8 + 10$,

$3x \leq 18$

$3x \leq 18$ (add 1 both side)

$3x + 1 \leq 18 + 1$

$3x + 1 \leq 19$

Largest possible value of 3x+1 is 19.

Correct Answer : E

13. Since x >0, then

|x| = x

|–2x| = 2x

|–3x| = 3x

So, $\frac{|x| + |-2x|}{|-3x|} = \frac{x + (2x)}{3x} = \frac{3x}{3x} = 1$

Correct Answer : C

14. Use prime factorization to find the greatest prime factor of 26 and 55.

If x is the greatest prime factor of 26, then 26 = 2.13 and the greatest prime factor of 26 is 13. (x = 13)

If y is the greatest prime factor of 55, then 55 = 5.11 and the greatest prime factor of 55 is 11. (y = 11)

x + y = 13 + 11 = 24

Correct Answer : C

15. Since the population of a City increased from 270 thousand to 360 thousand

Percent of increase:

$$\frac{360 - 270}{270} = \frac{90}{270} = \frac{9}{27} = \frac{1}{3} = 33.\overline{3}\%$$

Correct Answer : C

CHAPTER II HEART OF ALGEBRA
Linear Equations, System of Equations & Lines Test 6

1. If $4x - ay + 10 = 0$ and the slope of the equation is 1/5, then what is the value of a?

   A) 10
   B) 15
   C) 20
   D) 25
   E) 30

2. $$x + 4ky = 10$$
   $$5x - 12y = 12$$

   In the system of equations above, k is a constant. For what value of k will the system of equations have no solutions?

   A) $\frac{-3}{5}$
   B) $\frac{3}{5}$
   C) $\frac{-5}{3}$
   D) $\frac{-1}{5}$
   E) 5

3. If $x^2 + ax - 15 = (x - 1)(bx + c)$, then find b + c.

   A) 12
   B) 13
   C) 14
   D) 15
   E) 16

4. If the equation $\frac{20x^2}{2x-1}$ is written in the form $k + \frac{5}{2x-1}$ which of the following gives k in terms of x?

   A) $10 - 5x$
   B) $10x + 5$
   C) $5x + 10$
   D) $5x - 10$
   E) $5x - 15$

5. $\frac{2x-8}{3} - \frac{x+4}{4} = \frac{3}{2}$, find the value of x.

   A) 12.2
   B) 12.3
   C) 12.4
   D) 15.4
   E) 16.8

6. Write the equation in slope – intercept form for the line that passes through the points (–4, 4) and (2, –6).

   A) $y = -\frac{5}{3}x - \frac{8}{3}$
   B) $y = \frac{5}{3}x + \frac{32}{3}$
   C) $y = -\frac{5}{3}x - \frac{32}{3}$
   D) $y = -\frac{5}{3}x + \frac{22}{3}$
   E) $y = -\frac{5}{3}x + \frac{19}{3}$

Linear Equations, System of Equations & Lines Test 6

7. $\begin{cases} \frac{2}{3}x + \frac{3}{4}y = 12 \\ \frac{1}{3}x + \frac{3}{2}y = 18 \end{cases}$

   In the system of equations above, solve for the y value.

   A) 3
   B) 32
   C) $\frac{3}{32}$
   D) $\frac{32}{3}$
   E) 42

8. If $\frac{1}{2}x - ay - 8 = 0$ and the slope of the equations is $\frac{2}{7}$, then what is the value of a?

   A) 4
   B) 7
   C) $\frac{7}{4}$
   D) $\frac{4}{7}$
   E) $\frac{9}{4}$

9. If $\frac{1}{2}x - \frac{2}{3}y = 20$ and $y = 15$, then find x.

   A) 20
   B) 30
   C) 40
   D) 50
   E) 60

10. On the xy coordinate grid, a line K contains the points (1, 4) and (–1, 7). If the line L is parallel to line K at (3, 1), which of following is the equation of line L?

    A) $y = -\frac{3}{2}x + \frac{11}{2}$
    B) $y = \frac{3}{2}x + \frac{11}{2}$
    C) $y = -\frac{11}{2}x + \frac{3}{2}$
    D) $y = \frac{11}{2}x + \frac{3}{2}$
    E) $y = \frac{2}{11}x + \frac{3}{2}$

11. $x - 2ky = 7$
    $2x + 5y = 15$

    In the system of equations above, k is a constant. For what value of k will the system equations have no solutions?

    A) $\frac{5}{4}$
    B) $-\frac{5}{4}$
    C) $\frac{1}{2}$
    D) $-\frac{1}{2}$
    E) $-\frac{2}{5}$

Linear Equations, System of Equations & Lines Test 6

12.
$$2a + 3b = 18$$
$$3b - 5a = 11$$

What is the value of a – b?

A) 3

B) 13

C) $-\dfrac{13}{3}$

D) $\dfrac{13}{3}$

E) –13

13. In the xy – plane, the point (3, 5) lies on the graph of the function h. If $h(x) = x^2 - c$, where c is a constant, what is the value of c?

A) 0

B) 1

C) 2

D) 3

E) 4

14. Simplify $\dfrac{x^2 - 8x + 15}{x^2 - 9} \div \dfrac{x^2 - 4x - 5}{x^2 + 3x}$

A) x – 1

B) $\dfrac{x}{x+1}$

C) x + 1

D) $\dfrac{x+1}{x-1}$

E) x + 2

15.
$$k - 9 + \dfrac{5k}{2} = \dfrac{1}{2}k + 7$$

What is the value of k in the equation shown above?

A) $\dfrac{2}{5}$

B) $\dfrac{5}{8}$

C) $\dfrac{4}{17}$

D) $\dfrac{3}{16}$

E) $\dfrac{16}{3}$

16. A fitness center has two membership plans One is a $23 membership fee and $7 per visit and another one is only per visit fee of $13. Which of the following systems of equations can be used to determine the fitness center membership plans?

A) y = 7 + 23x
   y = 13

B) y = 23 + 7x
   y = 13x

C) y = 13
   y = 23 + 7x

D) y = 13x
   y = 23x + 7

E) y = 13
   y = 7x – 23

Linear Equations, System of Equations & Lines Test 6

17. Simplify $\dfrac{x^2y + xy^2 - xy}{x^2 + xy - x}$

A) x

B) y

C) 2xy

D) –x

E) –y

18. For a > 5, which of the following is equivalent to

$$\dfrac{1}{\dfrac{1}{x+3} + \dfrac{1}{x+5}} = ?$$

A) $\dfrac{2x+8}{x^2+8x+15}$

B) $\dfrac{x^2+8x+15}{2x+8}$

C) $\dfrac{2x+8}{x^2-8x+15}$

D) $x^2 + 8x + 15$

E) $x^2 - 8x - 15$

19. Find the distance between the two following two points.

(9, 7) and (7, 3)

A) 2

B) $\sqrt{2}$

C) $3\sqrt{2}$

D) 4

E) $2\sqrt{5}$

20. Calculate the midpoint of segment with the given endpoint:

(9, 7) and (7, 3)

A) (7, 3)

B) (9, 3)

C) (9, 7)

D) (5, 8)

E) (8, 5)

Linear Equations, System of Equations & Lines Test 6
Answer Key

1)	C
2)	A
3)	E
4)	B
5)	C
6)	A
7)	D
8)	C
9)	E
10)	A
11)	B
12)	C
13)	E
14)	B
15)	E
16)	B
17)	B
18)	B
19)	E
20)	E

Linear Equations, System of Equations & Lines Test 6
Solutions

1. $4x - ay + 10 = 0$ and $m = \dfrac{1}{5}$

    Slope of equation: $\dfrac{4}{a}$

    $\dfrac{1}{5} = \dfrac{4}{a}$, then $a = 20$

    Correct Answer : C

2. $x + 4ky = 10$

    $5x - 12y = 18$

    If a system has no solution, then $m_1 = m_2$

    $\dfrac{-1}{4k} = \dfrac{5}{12} \Rightarrow 20k = -12$, then $k = \dfrac{-12}{20} = \dfrac{-3}{5}$

    Correct Answer : A

3. $x^2 + ax - 15 = (x - 1)(bx + c) = (x - 1)(bx + c)$

    $x^2 + ax - 15 = bx^2 + cx - bx - c$

    $x^2 = b \cdot 2$, then $b = 1$

    $-15 = -c$, then $c = 15$

    $b + c = 1 + 15 = 16$

    Correct Answer : E

4. $\overline{}\,10x + 5$
    $2x - 1 \overline{\smash{)}20x^2}$
    $\underline{-20x^2 \pm 10x}$
    $10x$
    $\underline{-10x \pm 5}$
    5

    $k + \dfrac{5}{2x-1} = 10x + 5 + \dfrac{5}{2x-1}$

    $k = 10x + 5$

    Correct Answer : B

5. $\dfrac{2x-8}{3} - \dfrac{x+4}{4} = \dfrac{3}{2}$

    $\dfrac{4(2x-8)}{12} - \dfrac{3(x+4)}{12} = \dfrac{3 \cdot 6}{12}$

    $\dfrac{8x-32}{12} - \dfrac{3x+4}{12} = \dfrac{18}{12}$ (Cancel denominator)

    $8x - 32 - (3x - 12) = 18$

    $8x - 3x - 32 - 12 = 18$

    $5x - 44 = 18$

    $5x = 44 + 18$

    $5x = 62$

    $x = 12 \cdot 4$

    Correct Answer : C

6. Slope of two points:

    $m = \dfrac{y_2 - y_1}{x_2 - x_1}$

    $m = \dfrac{-6 - (4)}{2 - (-4)} = \dfrac{-10}{6} = -\dfrac{5}{3}$

    $y = mx + b$ (slope intercept form)

    Use $(-4, 4)$ to find b.

    $4 = -\dfrac{5}{3}(-4) + b$

    $4 = \dfrac{20}{3} + b$

    $4 - \dfrac{20}{3} = b$

    $-\dfrac{8}{3} = b$

    $y = -\dfrac{5}{3}x - \dfrac{8}{3}$

    Correct Answer : A

Linear Equations, System of Equations & Lines Test 6
Solutions

7. $\frac{2}{3}x + \frac{3}{4}y = 12$ $\frac{2}{3}x + \frac{3}{4}y = 12$
$-2\cdot\left(\frac{1}{3}x + \frac{3}{2}y = 18\right)$ $\cancel{\frac{-2}{3}}x - 3y = -36$

$\frac{3}{4}y - 3y = -24$

$\frac{-9y}{4} = -24$

$\frac{9y}{4} = 24$, $y = \frac{4\cdot 24}{9}$

$y = \frac{32}{3}$

Correct Answer : D

8. $\frac{1}{2}x - ay = 8$

slope intercept form $y = mx + b$

$\frac{1}{2}x - 8 = ay$

$\frac{1}{2a}x - \frac{8}{a} = y$ slope $= \frac{1}{2a}$

$\frac{1}{2a} = \frac{2}{7}$, $4a = 7$

$a = \frac{7}{4}$

Correct Answer : C

9. $\frac{1}{2}x - \frac{2}{3}y = 20$, $y = 15$

$\frac{1}{2}x - \frac{2}{3}(15) = 20$

$\frac{1}{2}x - \frac{30}{3} = 20$

$\frac{1}{2}x - 10 = 20$

$\frac{1}{2}x = 30$

$x = 60$

Correct Answer : E

10. Line K contains the points (1, 4) and (–1, 7).
Slope of point K
$m = \frac{y_2 - y_1}{x_2 - x_1} = \frac{7-4}{-1-(1)} = \frac{3}{-2} = -\frac{3}{2}$

Since line K is parallel to line L slopes are same.
Slope of point L is $-\frac{3}{2}$.
Slope – intercept form
$y = mx + b$
$y = -\frac{3}{2}x + b$ (use one of the above points to find b constant)

$7 = -\frac{3}{2}(-1) + b$

$7 = \frac{3}{2} + b$

$7 - \frac{3}{2} = b$

$\frac{11}{2} = b$

Equation of line L $\longrightarrow$ $y = -\frac{3}{2}x + \frac{11}{2}$

Correct Answer : A

Linear Equations, System of Equations & Lines Test 6
Solutions

11. If the systems of equations have no solutions, that means equations have the same slope.

$$x - 2ky = 7$$
$$2x + 5y = 15$$

NOTE: slope is a number next to the x over a number next to the y and sign is always opposite.

Slope of 1st equation is : $\frac{1}{2k}$

Slope of 2nd equation is : $-\frac{2}{5}$

Since slopes are equal.

$$\frac{1}{2k} = -\frac{2}{5}$$
$$-4k = 5$$
$$k = -\frac{5}{4}$$

Correct Answer : B

12. $2a + 3b = 18 \longrightarrow$ Multiply by(–)then use the elemenation method to find a and b.

$-2a - 3b = -18$
$3b - 5a = 11$
$+$ ─────────
$-7a = -7$

a = 1. Plug in one of the above equations and find b.

$2(1) + 3b = 18$
$2 + 3b = 18$
$3b = 16$
$b = 16/3$
$a - b = 1 - \frac{16}{3} = \frac{-13}{3}$

Correct Answer : C

13. $h(x) = x^2 - c$,(3,5) $\longrightarrow$ plug in this point to function for find c.

$h(3) = 3^2 - c$
$5 = 9 - c$
$c = 9 - 5$
$c = 4$

Correct Answer : E

14. $\dfrac{x^2 - 8x + 15}{x^2 - 9} \div \dfrac{x^2 - 4x - 5}{x^2 + 3x}$

$\dfrac{(x-5)(x-3)}{(x-3)(x+3)} \cdot \dfrac{x(x+3)}{(x-5)(x+1)}$

$= \dfrac{x}{x+1}$

Correct Answer : B

15. $k - 9 + \dfrac{5k}{2} = \dfrac{1}{2}k + 7$

$\dfrac{7k}{2} - 9 = \dfrac{1}{2}k + 7$

$\dfrac{7k}{2} - \dfrac{1}{2}k = 7 + 9$

$\dfrac{6k}{2} = 16$

$3k = 16$

$k = \dfrac{16}{3}$

Correct Answer : E

Linear Equations, System of Equations & Lines Test 6
Solutions

16. First plan: $23 membership fee and $7 per visit → convert to the equation.

y = $23 + 7x

Second plan: per visit fee of $13 → convert to the equation.

y = 13x (no membership fee)

Correct Answer : B

17. $\dfrac{x^2y + xy^2 - xy}{x^2 + xy - x}$

$\dfrac{xy\cancel{(x+y-1)}}{x\cancel{(x+y-1)}}$

$= \dfrac{xy}{x} = y$

Correct Answer : B

18. $\dfrac{1}{\dfrac{1}{x+3} + \dfrac{1}{x+5}} =$

$\dfrac{1}{\dfrac{(x+5)}{(x+3)\cdot(x+5)} + \dfrac{(x+3)}{(x+5)\cdot(x+3)}} =$

$\dfrac{1}{\dfrac{2x+8}{x^2+5x+3x+15}} = \dfrac{x^2+8x+15}{2x+8}$

Correct Answer : B

19. $|AB|^2 = (x_2 - x_1)^2 + (y_2 - y_1)^2$

$|AB| = \sqrt{(x_2-x_1)^2 + (y_2-y_1)^2}$

$AB = \sqrt{(9-7)^2 + (7-3)^2}$

$AB = \sqrt{(2)^2 + (4)^2}$

$AB = \sqrt{(4+16)}$

$AB = \sqrt{20} = 2\sqrt{5}$

Correct Answer : E

20. $x_0 = \dfrac{x_1 + x_2}{2} = \dfrac{9+7}{2} = \dfrac{16}{2} = 8$

$y_0 = \dfrac{y_1 + y_2}{2} = \dfrac{7+3}{2} = \dfrac{10}{2} = 5$

$x_0, y_0 = (8, 5)$

Correct Answer : E

Functions Test 8

1.
$$y = mx^2 + 3x + k$$

The graph of the function above has a y-intercept at y = –2 and an x-intercept at x = 2. What is the value of m?

A) 1

B) 0

C) –1

D) –2

E) –3

2.
$$f(x) = mx^2 + k$$

In the function above, m and k are constants. f(0) = 3, and f(2) = 7. What is the value of $f\left(\frac{-1}{2}\right)$?

A) 4

B) 13

C) $\frac{13}{4}$

D) $\frac{4}{13}$

E) 18

3. If $f(x) = x^2 + 2kx + c$ and the vertex point V is (1, 5), then find k + c.

A) 2

B) 4

C) 5

D) 8

E) 10

4. $f(x) = (x - 4)^2 + 11$

The function g is defined by g(x) = 2x + 2
What is one possible value such that f(a) = g(a)?

A) 3

B) 5

C) 7

D) 9

E) 10

58

Functions Test 8

5.

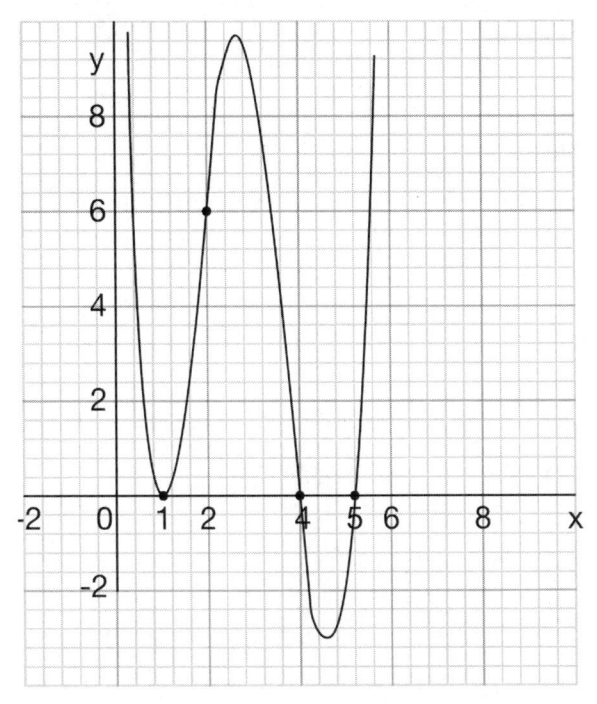

The function $y = f(x)$ is graphed in the xy coordinate plane above. Which of the following equations could describe $f(x)$?

A) $f(x) = (x - 1)^2 \cdot (x - 4) \cdot (x - 5)$

B) $f(x) = (x + 1)^2 \cdot (x - 4) \cdot (x - 5)$

C) $f(x) = (x - 1)^2 \cdot (x + 4) \cdot (x - 5)$

D) $f(x) = (x + 1)^2 \cdot (x + 4) \cdot (x + 5)$

E) $f(x) = (x - 1)^2 \cdot (x - 3) \cdot (x + 4)$

6. The range of the polynomial function f is the set of real numbers less than or equal to 2. If the zeros of f are –5 and 3, which of the following could be the graph of $y = f(x)$ in the xy–plane?

A)

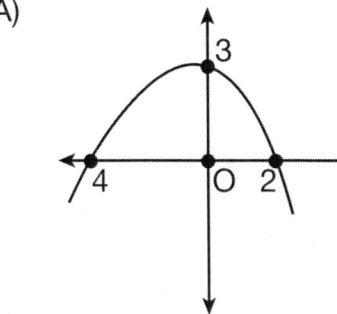

B)

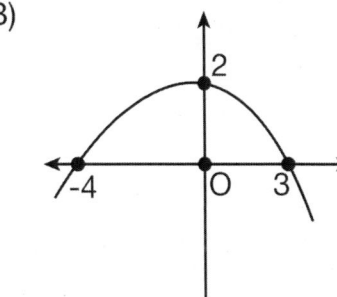

C)

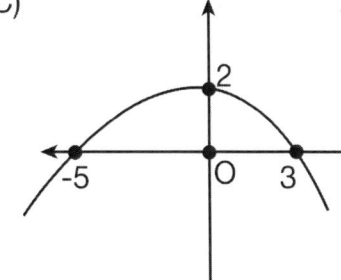

D)

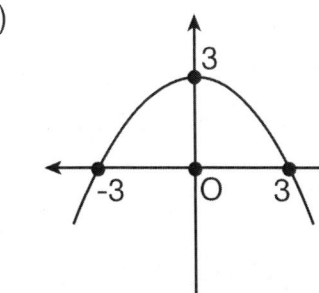

59

Functions Test 8

7. $f(x) = ax^2 + bx + c$.

If the function above has roots at –2, –5 and (3,1) is satisfied by the function, find a and b?

A) $a = \dfrac{1}{40}$ $b = \dfrac{7}{40}$

B) $a = \dfrac{3}{40}$ $b = \dfrac{5}{40}$

C) $a = \dfrac{5}{40}$ $b = \dfrac{7}{40}$

D) $a = \dfrac{1}{40}$ $b = \dfrac{5}{40}$

E) $a = \dfrac{1}{20}$ $b = \dfrac{1}{40}$

8.

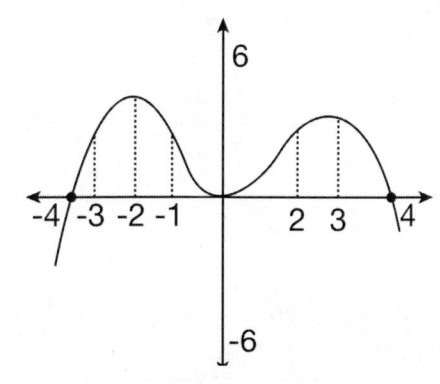

Which of the following could be the equation of the graph above?

A) $x \cdot (x - 3) \cdot (x + 3)$

B) $x^2 \cdot (x + 4) \cdot (x - 5)$

C) $x^2 \cdot (x - 4) \cdot (x + 4)$

D) $x^2 \cdot (x + 4) \cdot (x - 3)$

E) $x^2 \cdot (x + 4) \cdot (x + 4)$

9.

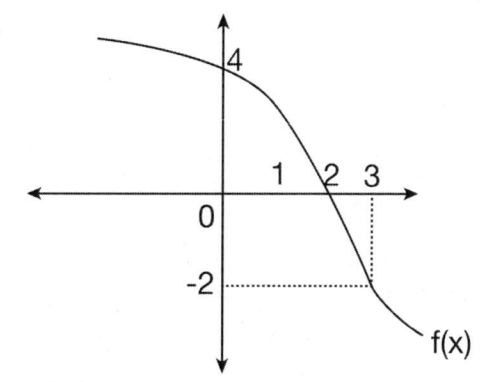

Using the above f(x) function, find the value of $f(0) + f^{-1}(-2) + f(3)$?

A) 5

B) 10

C) 12

D) 16

E) 18

10. What is the vertex of the parabola $y = 3x^2 + 6x - 9$?

A) $f(x) = 3(x + 1)^2 - 12$

B) $f(x) = 3(x + 1)^2 - 6$

C) $f(x) = 3(x - 1)^2 - 4$

D) $f(x) = 3(x - 1)^2 - 9$

D) $f(x) = 3(x - 1)^2 - 12$

Functions Test 8

11. In the xy–plane, the graph of function g(x) has x–intercepts at 2, 0, and –4.

Which of the following could define g(x)?

A) $3x^3 - 6x^2 + 24x$

B) $3x^3 + 12x^2 + 24x$

C) $3x^3 + 6x^2 - 24x$

D) $3x^3 - 12x^2 - 24x$

E) $3x^3 - 18x^2 - 24x$

12. In the xy–plane, the point (3, 5) lies on the graph of the function h. If $h(x) = x^2 - c$, where c is a constant, what is the value of c?

A) 1

B) 2

C) 3

D) 4

E) 5

13. $f(x) = \begin{cases} -2x+3, & x<0 \\ x^2+4, & x\geq 0 \end{cases}$

From the above function, find f(1) + f(–2)?

A) 7

B) 8

C) 9

D) 12

E) 15

14. The function $f(x) = (x - 3)(x - 5)(x + 8)$ will intersect the x–axis how many times?

A) 0

B) 1

C) 2

D) 3

E) 4

Functions Test 8

15. For the function below, m > 0 is a constant and f(2) = 20. What is the value of f(5)?

$$f(x) = mx^2 - 4$$

A) 146

B) 152

C) 154

D) 174

E) 178

16. The linear function g(x) is shown in the table below. Which of following defines g(x)?

x	g(x)
1	15
2	17
3	19

A) 2x + 10

B) 2x + 13

C) 2x − 13

D) 2x + 5

E) 2x + 12

17. Which of the following parabola functions could represent the graph in the picture?

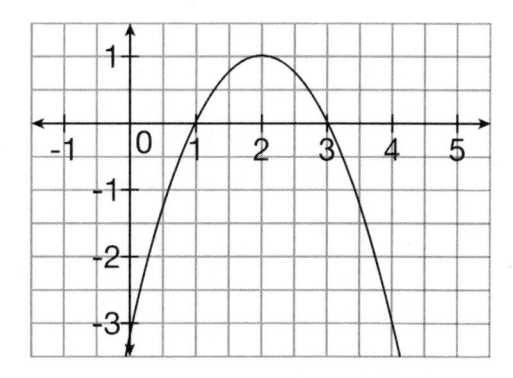

A) $f(x) = -x^2 + 4x + 3$

B) $f(x) = -x^2 - 4x + 3$

C) $f(x) = -x^2 - 4x - 3$

D) $f(x) = -x^2 + 4x - 3$

E) $f(x) = -x^2 + 4x - 6$

62

Functions Test 8
Answer Key

1)	C
2)	C
3)	C
4)	B
5)	A
6)	C
7)	A
8)	C
9)	A
10)	A
11)	C
12)	D
13)	D
14)	D
15)	A
16)	B
17)	D

Functions Test 8
Solutions

1.
$y = mx^2 + 3x + k$

y-intercept at $y = -2$, $x = 0$
$-2 = m \cdot 0^2 + 3 \cdot 0 + k$
$-2 = k$

x-intercept at $x = 2$, $y = 0$
$0 = m \cdot 2^2 + 3 \cdot 2 + k$
$0 = 4m + 6 + k$
$0 = 4m + 6 - 2$
$0 = 4m + 4$
$-4 = 4m$
$-1 = m$

Correct Answer : C

2. $f(x) = mx^2 + k$
$f(0) = 3$
$f(0) = m \cdot 0^2 + k$
$3 = 0 + k$
$3 = k$
$f(x) = mx^2 + 3$
$f(2) = m \cdot 2^2 + 3$
$7 = 4m + 3$
$4 = 4m$
$1 = m$
$f(x) = x^2 + 3$
$f\left(-\dfrac{1}{2}\right) = \left(-\dfrac{1}{2}\right)^2 + 3$
$= \dfrac{1}{4} + 3$
$= \dfrac{13}{4}$

Correct Answer : C

3. $f(x) = x^2 + 2kx + c$

$x = \dfrac{-b}{2a}$ (Axis of symmetry)

$x = \dfrac{-b}{2a}$

$x = \dfrac{-2k}{2}$

$1 = \dfrac{-2k}{2}$ (since x = 1)

$2 = -2k$

$-1 = k$

V(1, 5) ⟶ plug this point in to the equation

$5 = 1^2 + 2k(1) + c$
$4 = 2k + c$, $k = -1$
$4 = 2(-1) + c$
$4 + 2 = c$
$6 = c$
$k + c = 6 + (-1) = 5$

Correct Answer : C

4. $f(a) = (a - 4)^2 + 11$
$g(a) = 2a + 2$
If $f(a) = g(a) \implies (a - 4)^2 + 11 = 2a + 2$
$a^2 - 8a + 16 + 11 = 2a + 2$
$a^2 - 8a + 27 = 2a + 2$
$a^2 - 10a + 25 = 0$
$(a - 5)^2 = 0$
$a = 5$

Correct Answer : B

Functions Test 8
Solutions

5. Since the graph has x – intercepts at x = 1, x = 4 and x = 5, then by the Factor They are the polynomid must have factors of (x – 1) . (x – 4) . (x – 5)

Also, the graph contains the point (2, 6).

This point satisfies the function in choice A.

Correct Answer : A

6. (0, 2) is satisfied and

x = –5 and x = 3

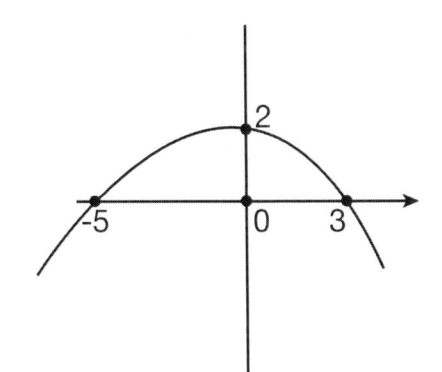

Correct Answer : C

7. $f(x) = t(x + 2) \cdot (x + 5)$, and (3, 1) is satisfied that;

$1 = t(3 + 2) \cdot (3 + 5)$

$1 = t \cdot (5) \cdot (8)$

$1 = t \cdot 40$

$t = \dfrac{1}{40}$

So;

$f(x) = \dfrac{1}{40} \cdot (x + 2) \cdot (x + 5)$

$\Longrightarrow \dfrac{1}{40} \cdot (x^2 + 7x + 10)$

$\Longrightarrow \dfrac{x^2}{40} + \dfrac{7x}{40} + \dfrac{1}{4} = ax^2 + bx + c$

$a = \dfrac{1}{40}, b = \dfrac{7}{40}$

Correct Answer : A

8. The graph's zeros are x = 0, x = 4, x = –4 but x = 0 in twice times so;

$f(x) = x^2 \cdot (x - 4) \cdot (x + 4)$

$= x^2 \cdot (x^2 - 16)$

Correct Answer : C

9. $f(0) = 4$

$f^{-1}(-2) = 3$, then $f(3) = -2$

$f(0) + f^{-1}(2) + f(3) = 4 + 3 - 2 = 5$

Correct Answer : A

Functions Test 8
Solutions

10. $y = 3x^2 + 6x - 9$

$y = 3(x^2 + 2x) + 9$

$y = 3(x + 1)^2 - 3 - 9$

$y = 3(x + 1)^2 - 12$

Correct Answer : A

11. If the g(x) function has x– intercept at 2, 0, and –4, then x – 2, x and x + 4 must be factor of g(x).

$g(x) = kx(x - 2)(x + 4) \longrightarrow$ which k is a constant

$g(x) = kx(x^2 + 2x - 8) \longrightarrow$ FOIL

$g(x) = k(x^3 + 2x^2 - 8x) \longrightarrow$ Distributive property

Since the leading coefficient is 3 in each answer choice, k must be 3.

$g(x) = 3(x^3 + 2x^2 - 8x)$

$g(x) = 3x^3 + 6x^2 - 24x$

Correct Answer : C

12. $h(x) = x^2 - c$, (3,5) $\longrightarrow$ plug in this point to function for find c.

$h(3) = 3^2 - c$

$5 = 9 - c$

$c = 9 - 5$

$c = 4$

Correct Answer : D

13. $f(x) = x^2 + 4$, when $x \geq 0$

$f(1) = 1^2 + 4 = 5$

$f(x) = -x + 5$, when $x < 0$

$f(-2) = -(-2) + 5 = 2 + 5 = 7$

$f(1) + f(-2) = 5 + 7 = 12$

Correct Answer : D

14. $f(x) = (x - 3)(x - 5)(x + 8)$

$x - 3 = 0, x = 3$

$x - 5 = 0, x = 5$

$x + 8 = 0, x = -8$

Correct Answer : D

15. $f(2) = 20$

$f(x) = mx^2 - 4$

$f(2) = 2^2 \cdot m - 4$

$20 = 4m - 4$

$20 + 4 = 4m$

$24 = 4m$

$6 = m$

$f(x) = 6x^2 - 4$

$f(5) = 6 \cdot 5^2 - 4$

$f(5) = 6 \cdot 25 - 4$

$f(5) = 150 - 4$

$f(5) = 146$

Correct Answer : A

Functions Test 8
Solutions

16. Linear function $g(x) = mx + b$

Slope $= \dfrac{y_2 - y_1}{x_2 - x_1} = \dfrac{17 - 15}{2 - 1} = \dfrac{2}{1} = 2$

$g(x) = 2x + b$, use any point from the table to find b.

$15 = 2(1) + b$

$15 - 2 = b$

$b = 13$

$g(x) = 2x + 13$

Correct Answer : B

17. From the graph the vertex points are (2,1).

$V(x) = a(x - h)^2 + k$

$V(x) = a(x - 2)^2 + 1$

From the graph you can use (0, –3)

$-3 = a(a - 2)^2 + 1$

$-3 = 4a + 1$

$-4 = 4a$, $a = -1$

$V(x) = -(x - 2)^2 + 1$

$V(x) = -(x^2 - 4x + 4) + 1$

$= -x^2 + 4x - 4 + 1$

$= -x^2 + 4x - 3$

Correct Answer : D

Statistics & Probability Test 9

1. If a is the average of 2k and 2, b is the average of 4k and 8, and c is the average 6k and 20, then what is the average of a, b, and c in terms of k?

   A) k

   B) 2k

   C) 2k − 5

   D) 2k + 5

   E) 2k − 7

2. A letter is chosen at random from the word "mathematician." What is the probability of choosing either an A or I?

   A) $\frac{5}{13}$

   B) $\frac{4}{13}$

   C) $\frac{13}{5}$

   D) 13

   E) 18

Use the following chart to answer questions 3 to 5

	With glasses	No glasses
Girl	10	6
Boy	6	12

The chart is about the students in the class and their situation with glasses.

3. What is the probability that the selected student has no glasses?

   A) $\frac{8}{17}$

   B) $\frac{9}{17}$

   C) $\frac{10}{17}$

   D) $\frac{21}{34}$

   E) $\frac{17}{10}$

4. What is the probability that the selected student is a girl?

   A) $\frac{8}{17}$

   B) $\frac{9}{17}$

   C) $\frac{11}{17}$

   D) $\frac{12}{17}$

   E) $\frac{13}{17}$

Statistics & Probability Test 9

5. What is the probability of the selected student is no glasses and girls?

A) $\dfrac{1}{17}$

B) $\dfrac{2}{17}$

C) $\dfrac{3}{17}$

D) $\dfrac{4}{17}$

E) $\dfrac{5}{17}$

6. If a is the average of 8k and 10, b is the average of 6k and 10, and c is the average of 10k and 40, what is the average of a, b, and c in terms of k?

A) 4k + 20

B) 4k − 15

C) 4k + 15

D) 4k + 10

E) 4k − 20

7. The temperature in Celsius (C°) in the first week of October was as follow:

25C°, 21C°, 20C°, 25C°, 23C°, 14C°, 32C°

What is the mode of the temperatures for the first week of October?

A) 20C°

B) 21C°

C) 23C°

D) 25C°

E) 30C°

8. What measure of central tendency is calculated by a difference between the lowest and highest the number of values?

A) Median

B) Mean

C) Mode

D) Range

E) None of above

9. The average of five consecutive positive integers is 28. What is the greatest possible value of one of these integers?

A) 24

B) 26

C) 30

D) 32

E) 34

Statistics & Probability Test 9

10. Two classes have taken a science test. The first class had 20 students and the average test score of that class was 90%. The second class had 24 students and their average score was 85%. If the teacher combined the test scores of both classes, what is the average of both classes together if you round your answer to the nearest ones?

A) 82%

B) 83%

C) 86%

D) 87%

E) 92%

11. What is the median score achieved by a class who recorded the following scores on 6 science tests?

74, 80, 78, 65, 90, 92

A) 76

B) 77

C) 78

D) 79

E) 82

Use the data to answer question 12

The temperature in Celsius (C°) in the first week of October was a follows.

25C°, 21C°, 20C°, 25C°, 23C°, 14C°, 32C°

12. From the above data, what is the range of the temperatures for the first week of October?

A) 12C°

B) 16C°

C) 18C°

D) 21C°

E) 23C°

Statistics & Probability Test 9
Answer Key

1)	D
2)	A
3)	B
4)	A
5)	C
6)	D
7)	D
8)	D
9)	C
10)	D
11)	D
12)	C

Statistics & Probability Test 9
Solutions

1. $a = \dfrac{2k+2}{2} = k+1$

$b = \dfrac{4k+8}{2} = 2k+4$

$c = \dfrac{6k+20}{2} = 3k+10$

Average of a, b and c

$\dfrac{a+b+c}{3} = \dfrac{k+1+2k+4+3k+10}{3}$

$= \dfrac{6k+15}{3} = 2k+5$

Correct Answer : D

2. Probability of A or I

total amount of A's = 3

total amount of I's = 2

$\dfrac{\text{total A and I}}{\text{total letters}} = \dfrac{5}{13}$

Correct Answer : A

3. Number of students with no glasses = $\dfrac{18}{34} = \dfrac{9}{17}$

Correct Answer : B

4. Probability that the selected student is a girl

$= \dfrac{16}{34} = \dfrac{8}{17}$

Correct Answer : A

5. Probability that the selected student does not glasses and are girls

$= \dfrac{6}{34} = \dfrac{3}{17}$

Correct Answer : C

6. $a = \dfrac{8k+10}{2} = 4k+5$

$b = \dfrac{6k+10}{2} = 3k+5$

$c = \dfrac{10k+40}{2} = 5k+20$

Average of a, b, and c = $\dfrac{a+b+c}{3}$

$= \dfrac{4k+5+3k+5+5k+20}{3}$

$= \dfrac{12k+30}{3} = 4k+15$

Correct Answer : D

7. Mode: The mode is the most frequent value. From the data the correct answer is 25C°

Correct Answer : D

8. Range means the difference between the lowest and highest number values.

Correct Answer : D

Statistics & Probability Test 9
Solutions

9. $\dfrac{x + x+1 + x+2 + x+3 + x+4}{5} = 28$

$\dfrac{5x + 10}{5} = 28$

$x + 2 = 28$

$x = 26$

The greatest one $= x + 4$
$= 26 + 4$
$= 30$

Correct Answer : C

10. $\dfrac{\text{sum}}{\text{\# of students}} = .90$

$\dfrac{\text{sum}}{20} = .90$, sum $= 18$

$\dfrac{\text{sum}}{\text{\# of students}} = .85$

$\dfrac{\text{sum}}{24} = .85$, sum $= 20 \cdot 4$

total sum $= 18 + 40.4 = 38.4$

total students $= 20 + 24 = 44$

Estimated Average $= \dfrac{38 \cdot 4}{44}$

$\cong .87$

$\cong 87\%$

Correct Answer : D

11. Median :

65, 74, 78, 80, 90, 92

$\dfrac{78 + 80}{2} = 79$

Correct Answer : D

12. Range = max − min

R = 32ºC − 14ºC

R = 18ºC

Correct Answer : C

Mixed Review Test II

1.

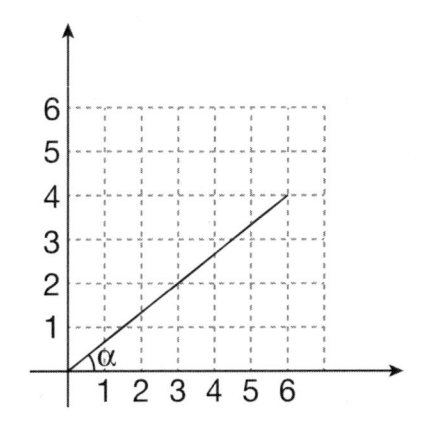

What is the equation of the function?

A) $y = 2x$

B) $y = \dfrac{2}{3}x$

C) $y = x + 7$

D) $y = 2x + 3$

E) $y = 3x + 2$

2. $ax^3 + bx^2 + cx + d = 0$

In the equation above, a,b,c and d are constants. If the equation roots are −2,4 and −7, which of the following is a factor of $ax^3 + bx^2 + cx + d$?

A) $x - 2$

B) $x + 4$

C) $x + 7$

D) $x - 7$

E) $x + 8$

3. A{0, 1, 2, 3, 4, 5, 6, 7, 8, 9}

What is the probability of selecting an even number in set A?

A) $\dfrac{1}{2}$

B) $\dfrac{3}{4}$

C) $\dfrac{5}{6}$

D) $\dfrac{2}{3}$

E) $\dfrac{3}{2}$

4. If $3y - \dfrac{x}{4} = 10$, then which of the following is equal to $\dfrac{x}{2}$?

A) $6y - 20$

B) $3y - 10$

C) $y - 20$

D) $6y + 20$

E) $y + 20$

5. If $x^{\frac{1}{3}} = 64$, then find $\dfrac{x}{2}$.

A) 2^{15}

B) 2^{17}

C) 2^{18}

D) 2^{20}

E) 2^{25}

74

Mixed Review Test II

6. If x, y and z are real numbers and;
$$x^3 \cdot y^2 > 0$$
$$x^2 \cdot z > 0$$
$$y^3 \cdot z < 0$$
Which of the following must be true?

A) +, +, +

B) −, +, −

C) +, −, −

D) +, −, +

E) −, −, +

7. Simplify $\sqrt{27} - \sqrt{81} + \sqrt{243}$.

A) $3\sqrt{3} - 9$

B) $6\sqrt{3} - 9$

C) $9\sqrt{3} - 9$

D) $12\sqrt{3} - 9$

E) $15\sqrt{3} - 9$

8. The price of a book has been discounted 20%. The sale price is $45. What is the original price?

A) $45.5

B) $51.5

C) $51.75

D) $56.25

E) $66.25

9. Find y when x = 3, if y varies directly as x and y = 20 when x = 5.

A) 6

B) 9

C) 12

D) 15

E) 18

10. If $\dfrac{a^2}{b^2} + \dfrac{b^2}{a^2} = 7$, then which of following could be $\dfrac{a}{b} + \dfrac{b}{a} = ?$

A) 1

B) 3

C) 2

D) −1

E) −2

11. Evaluate $4 + (2 + 3) \cdot 5 - 8 + (5 + 3)^0$?

A) 15

B) 16

C) 17

D) 22

E) 25

75

Mixed Review Test II

12. If $x > 0$ and $x - 3 = \sqrt{x-3}$, then which of following can be x?

A) 0

B) 1

C) 2

D) 4

E) 5

13. Solve $\dfrac{2}{2-\sqrt{2}}$.

A) 4

B) $-\sqrt{2}$

C) $2 + \sqrt{2}$

D) $2 - \sqrt{2}$

E) $1 + \sqrt{2}$

14. Simplify $\dfrac{1}{x-1} + \dfrac{1}{x+1}$.

A) $x - 1$

B) $x + 1$

C) 1

D) $\dfrac{2x}{x^2-1}$

E) x

15. Simplify $\dfrac{x^2-8x+15}{x^2-9} \div \dfrac{x^2-4x-5}{x^2+3x}$.

A) $x - 1$

B) $\dfrac{x}{x+1}$

C) $x + 1$

D) $\dfrac{x+1}{x-1}$

E) $\dfrac{x-2}{x+2}$

Mixed Review Test II
Answer Key

1)	B
2)	C
3)	A
4)	A
5)	B
6)	D
7)	D
8)	D
9)	C
10)	B
11)	D
12)	D
13)	C
14)	D
15)	B

Mixed Review Test II
Solutions

1. $\tan\alpha = \dfrac{2}{3}$

(0, 0) is satisfied

$y - 0 = \dfrac{2}{3}(x - 0)$

$y = \dfrac{2}{3}x$

Correct Answer : B

2. $f(x) = t(x + 2)(x - 4)(x + 7)$

So, $x + 7$ is a factor of $f(x)$

Correct Answer : C

3. Even numbers are 0, 2, 4, 6, and 8.

Probability of the selecting even number

$= \dfrac{5}{10} = \dfrac{1}{2}$

Correct Answer : A

4. $3y - \dfrac{x}{4} = 10$

$3y - 10 = \dfrac{x}{4} \longrightarrow$ multiply both sides by 2.

$2(3y - 10) = \dfrac{x}{4}(2)$

$6y - 20 = \dfrac{x}{2}$

Correct Answer : A

5. $x^{\frac{1}{3}} = 64$, then $x^{\frac{1}{3}} = 4^3 \longrightarrow$ multiply each power by 3 to find x

$x^{\frac{1(3)}{3}} = 4^{3(3)}$

$x = 4^9$

$\dfrac{x}{2} = \dfrac{4^9}{2^1} = \dfrac{(2^2)^9}{2^1} = \dfrac{2^{18}}{2^1} = 2^{18-1} = 2^{17}$

Correct Answer : B

6. If $x^3 \cdot y^2 > 0$ so y^2 is always positive then $x > 0$

If $x^2 \cdot z > 0$ so x^2 is always positive then $z > 0$

If $y^3 \cdot z < 0$ so we knows $z > 0$ then $y < 0$

Correct Answer : D

7. $= \sqrt{27} - \sqrt{81} + \sqrt{243}$

$= 3\sqrt{3} - 9 + 9\sqrt{3}$

$= 12\sqrt{3} - 9$

Correct Answer : D

8. Discount 20%

Orginal Price = 100x

Discount 20% = 20x

Sale Price = Original Price − Discount

$\$45 = 100x - 20x$

$45 = 80x$

$\dfrac{45}{80} = x$

$x = 56.25\$$

Correct Answer : D

Mixed Review Test II
Solutions

9. $y = k$
$20 = k \cdot 5$
$k = 4$
___
$y = kx$
$y = 4 \cdot 3$
$y = 12$

Correct Answer : C

10. $\dfrac{a^2}{b^2} + \dfrac{b^2}{a^2} = 7$, then
$\dfrac{a}{b} + \dfrac{b}{a} = ?$

$\left(\dfrac{a}{b} + \dfrac{b}{a}\right)^2 - 2 = 7$

$\left(\dfrac{a}{b} + \dfrac{b}{a}\right)^2 = 9$

$\dfrac{a}{b} + \dfrac{b}{a} = 3$

Correct Answer : B

11. $4 + (2 + 3) \cdot 5 - 8 + (5 + 3)^0$
$= 4 + 5 \cdot 5 - 8 + 1$
$= 4 + 25 - 8 + 1$
$= 29 - 8 + 1$
$= 21 + 1$
$= 22$

Correct Answer : D

12. $x - 3 = \sqrt{x - 3}$
$(x - 3)^2 = x - 3$
$x^2 - 6x + 9 = x - 3$
$x^2 - 7x + 12 = 0$
$(x - 3) \cdot (x - 4) = 0$
$x = 3 \text{ or } x = 4$

Correct Answer : D

13. Solve $\dfrac{2}{2 - \sqrt{2}}$

$= \dfrac{2(2 + \sqrt{2})}{(2 - \sqrt{2})(2 + \sqrt{2})}$

$= \dfrac{4 + 2\sqrt{2}}{4 - 2} = \dfrac{4 + 2\sqrt{2}}{2} = 2 + \sqrt{2}$

Correct Answer : C

14. $\dfrac{1}{x - 1} + \dfrac{1}{x + 1} = \dfrac{x + 1 + x - 1}{(x - 1)(x + 1)}$

$= \dfrac{2x}{(x - 1)(x + 1)}$

$= \dfrac{2x}{x^2 - 1}$

Correct Answer : D

15. $\dfrac{x^2 - 8x + 15}{x^2 - 9} \div \dfrac{x^2 - 4x - 5}{x^2 + 3x}$

$\dfrac{(x-5)(x-3)}{(x-3)(x+3)} \cdot \dfrac{x(x+3)}{(x-5)(x+1)}$

$= \dfrac{x}{x + 1}$

Correct Answer : B

CHAPTER III PASSPORT TO ADVANCED MATH
Polynomials Test 10

1. If $x^2 + ax - 10 = (x - 1)(bx + c)$, then find $b + c$.

   A) 50
   B) 10
   C) 11
   D) 12
   E) 15

2. If the equation $\dfrac{20x^2}{2x-1}$ is written in the form $k + \dfrac{5}{2x-1}$ which of the following gives k in terms of x?

   A) $10 - 5x$
   B) $10x + 5$
   C) $5x + 10$
   D) $5x - 10$
   E) $10x - 10$

3. If $P(x + 1) = 3x + 1$, then what is $P(x + 3)$?

   A) $2x + 7$
   B) $3x + 7$
   C) $-3x + 5$
   D) $2x + 1$
   E) $3x - 7$

4. If $P(x - 2) = x^2 + 2x + 1$, then find $P(x + 1)$?

   A) $x^2 + 8x + 16$
   B) $-x^2 + 8x + 16$
   C) $x^2 - 8x + 16$
   D) $x^2 + 8x - 16$
   E) $x^2 + 8x - 12$

5. $P(x - 2) = x^2 + 3x - 10$, then find $P(3)$.

   A) 10
   B) 20
   C) 30
   D) 40
   E) 45

6. In the polynomial below, a is the constant. If the polynomial $P(x)$ is divisible by $x+2$ then find the value of a.

   $$P(x) = 2x^3 + ax^2 - x + 2$$

   A) 2
   B) 3
   C) 5
   D) 7
   E) 9

Polynomials Test 10

7. $P(x) = 3x^3 - 7x^2 + 2$ and $Q(x) = 2x^3 + 2x^2 + 5$ Then find $P(x) - Q(x)$.

A) $x^3 - 9x^2 - 3$

B) $x^3 + 9x^2 - 3$

C) $x^3 - 9x^2 + 7$

D) $x^3 - 2x^2 - 7$

E) $x^3 + 9x^2 - 12$

8. $P(x) = 2x - 1$ and $Q(x) = 2x^3 + 2x^2 - 1$, then find $P(x) \cdot Q(x)$.

A) $4x^4 - 2x^3 - 2x^2 - 2x + 1$

B) $4x^4 + 2x^3 + 2x^2 - 2x + 1$

C) $4x^4 + 2x^3 - 2x^2 - 2x + 1$

D) $4x^4 - 2x^3 - 2x^2 + 2x - 1$

E) $4x^4 + 2x^3 - 2x^2 + 2x + 1$

9. Simplify $\dfrac{1}{x-1} + \dfrac{1}{x+1}$.

A) $x - 1$

B) $x + 1$

C) 1

D) $\dfrac{2x}{x^2-1}$

E) $x - 2$

10. Simplify $\dfrac{x^2 - 7x + 12}{x^2 - 9x + 20}$.

A) $\dfrac{x-3}{x-4}$

B) $\dfrac{x-3}{x-5}$

C) $\dfrac{x-4}{x-3}$

D) $\dfrac{x-5}{x-3}$

E) $\dfrac{x-3}{x-7}$

Polynomials Test 10

11. If A and B are real numbers then what is A + B?

$$\frac{2x+6}{x^2-1} = \frac{A}{x-1} + \frac{B}{x+1}$$

A) 2

B) 4

C) –2

D) –4

E) –5

12. Simplify $\dfrac{x^2-8x+15}{x^2-9} \div \dfrac{x^2-4x-5}{x^2+3x}$

A) x + 1

B) $\dfrac{x}{x+1}$

C) x + 1

D) $\dfrac{x+1}{x-1}$

E) 21

13. Simplify $\dfrac{x^2-y^2}{x^2+xy} \div \dfrac{x^2-xy}{xy+x}$.

A) x + 1

B) y + 1

C) $\dfrac{x+1}{y}$

D) $\dfrac{y+1}{x}$

E) x – 1

Polynomials Test 10
Answer Key

1)	C
2)	B
3)	B
4)	A
5)	C
6)	B
7)	A
8)	C
9)	D
10)	B
11)	A
12)	B
13)	D

Polynomials Test 10
Solutions

1. $x^2 + ax - 10 = (x-1)(bx + c)$
$x^2 + ax - 10 = bx^2 + cx - bx - c$
$bx^2 = x^2$, $b = 1$
$-10 = -c$, $c = 10$
$b + c = 11$

Correct Answer : C

2.
$$\begin{array}{r} 10x + 5 \\ 2x - 1 \overline{)20x^2} \\ -20x^2 \mp 10x \\ \hline 10x \\ -10x \pm 5 \\ \hline 5 \end{array}$$

$k + \dfrac{5}{2x-1} = 10x + 5 \; \dfrac{5}{2x-1}$

$k = 10x + 5$

Correct Answer : B

3. $P(x + 1) = 3x + 1$
$P(x + 2) + 1) = 3(x + 2) + 1$
$P(x + 3) = 3x + 6 + 1 = 3x + 7$

Correct Answer : B

4. $P(x - 2) = x^2 + 2x + 1$

To find P (x + 1) plug in x + 3 for x in P(x – 2).

$P(x + 3 - 2) = (x + 3)^2 + 2(x + 3) + 1$
$P(x + 1) = x^2 + 6x + 9 + 2x + 6 + 1$
$P(x + 1) = x^2 + 8x + 16$

Correct Answer : A

5. $P(x - 2) = x^2 + 3x - 10$, then plug 5 in x to find P(3).

$P(5 - 2) = 5^2 + 3(5) - 10$
$P(3) = 25 + 15 - 10$
$P(3) = 40 - 10$
$P(3) = 30$

Correct Answer : C

6. Since P(x) is divisible by x + 2
then x + 2 = 0
$x = -2$
$P(-2) = 0$
$P(-2) = 2 \cdot (-2)^3 + a(-2)^2 - (-2) + 2$
$P(-2) = -16 + 4a + 2 + 2$
$P(-2) = -12 + 4a$
$0 = -12 + 4a$
$12 = 4a \quad a = 3$

Correct Answer : B

84

Polynomials Test 10
Solutions

7. $P(x) - Q(x) = (3x^3 - 7x^2 + 2) - (2x^3 + 2x^2 + 5)$
$= x^3 - 9x^2 - 3$
Correct Answer : A

8. $P(x) \cdot Q(x)$
$(2x - 1) \cdot (2x^3 + 2x^2 - 1)$
$= 4x^4 + 4x^3 - 2x - 2x^3 - 2x^2 + 1$
$= 4x^4 + 2x^3 - 2x^2 - 2x + 1$
Correct Answer : C

9. $\dfrac{1}{x-1} + \dfrac{1}{x-1} = \dfrac{x+1+x-1}{(x-1)(x+1)}$
$= \dfrac{2x}{(x-1)(x+1)}$
$= \dfrac{2x}{x^2-1}$
Correct Answer : D

10. $\dfrac{x^2 - 7x + 12}{x^2 - 9x + 20} = \dfrac{(x-3) \cdot (x-4)}{(x-4) \cdot (x-5)}$
$= \dfrac{x-3}{x-5}$
Correct Answer : B

11. $\dfrac{2x+6}{x^2-1} = \dfrac{A}{x-1} + \dfrac{B}{x+1}$
$2x + 6 = A(x+1) + B(x-1)$
$2x + 6 = Ax + A + Bx - B$
$2x + 6 = x(A+B) + A - B$
$2x = x(A+B)$
$2 = A + B \quad 2A = 8, A = 4$
$6 = A - B \quad\quad B = -2$
$A + B = 4 - 2 = 2$
Correct Answer : A

12. $\dfrac{x^2 - 8x + 15}{x^2 - 9} \div \dfrac{x^2 - 4x - 5}{x^2 + 3x}$
$\dfrac{(x-5)(x-3)}{(x-3)(x+3)} \cdot \dfrac{x(x+3)}{(x-5)(x+1)}$
$= \dfrac{x}{x+1}$
Correct Answer : B

13. $\dfrac{x^2 - y^2}{x^2 + xy} \div \dfrac{x^2 - xy}{xy + x}$
$\dfrac{(x-y)(x+y)}{x(x+y)} \cdot \dfrac{x(y+1)}{x(x-y)}$
$\dfrac{y+1}{x}$
Correct Answer : D

85

Complex Numbers Test 11

1. $i^0 + i^{31} + i^{10}$

Which of the following is equivalent to the complex number shown above? ($i^2 = -1$)

A) i

B) –i

C) 2i

D) –2i

E) 1

2. Solve for x in the equation below:
$$x^2 + 4x + 5 = 0$$

A) $= 2 \mp i$

B) $= -2 \mp i$

C) $2 - i$

D) $2 + i$

E) $2i$

3. Which of the following complex numbers are equivalent to $\left(\dfrac{1+i}{1-i}\right)^{2018}$?

A) 1

B) –1

C) i

D) –i

E) 0

4. $i^{2019} + i^{2020} + i^{2021}$

Which of the following is equivalent to the complex number shown above?

A) i

B) 1

C) 2i

D) 2

E) 0

5. If $a = 1 - 5i$ and $b = 1 + 5i$, then which of the following is equal to $a \cdot b$?

A) 10

B) 15

C) 25

D) 26

E) 27

6. Which of the following is equal to $\dfrac{4}{1+i\sqrt{3}}$?

A) $1 - i\sqrt{3}$

B) $1 + i\sqrt{3}$

C) 1

D) 3i

E) –3i

86

Complex Numbers Test 11

7. Which of the following complex numbers are equivalent to $\dfrac{a-bi}{a+bi}$?

   A) $\dfrac{a^2-2abi+b^2}{a^2+b^2}$

   B) a^2+b^2

   C) $\dfrac{a^2-2abi+b^2}{a^2-b^2}$

   D) $\dfrac{a^2-2abi-b^2}{a^2+b^2}$

   E) $\dfrac{a^2-2abi+b^2}{a-b}$

8. Which of the following compex numbers are equivalent to $(i-2)(i+6)$

   A) $13+4i$

   B) $-13+4i$

   C) $4+13i$

   D) $4-13i$

   E) $13i-4$

9. What is the simplest form of $\sqrt{-5}\cdot\sqrt{75}$

   A) $5i\sqrt{15}$

   B) $5\sqrt{15}$

   C) 5

   D) $-5\sqrt{15}i$

   E) $5i$

10. $24=-4x^2$. Solve for x.

    A) $\pm i\sqrt{6}$

    B) $-i\sqrt{6}$

    C) $6i$

    D) -6

    E) $9i$

11. Which of the following complex numbers is equivalent to $\left(\dfrac{1}{2}-\dfrac{i}{2}\right)\cdot\left(\dfrac{1}{2}+\dfrac{i}{2}\right)$?

    A) $\dfrac{i}{2}$

    B) $\dfrac{2}{2i}$

    C) $\dfrac{1}{2}$

    D) $-\dfrac{1}{2}$

    E) i

12. Simplify $\sqrt{-5}+\sqrt{-20}+\sqrt{-125}$?

    A) $-8i\sqrt{5}$

    B) $8i\sqrt{5}$

    C) $8i$

    D) $-8i$

    E) 8

87

Complex Numbers Test 11

13. Which of the following is equivalent to the complex numbers $\frac{2}{3} - \frac{i}{6}$?

A) $\frac{4-i}{6}$

B) $\frac{6-i}{4}$

C) $\frac{4+i}{6}$

D) $\frac{6+i}{4}$

E) $6-i$

14. Which of the following complex numbers are equivalent to $\frac{4}{i} + i$?

A) $-3i$

B) $3i$

C) $\frac{i}{3}$

D) i

E) $-i$

15. $i^{2018} \cdot i^{2019}$

Which of the following is equivalent to the complex number shown above?

A) 0

B) 1

C) $-i$

D) i

E) $2i$

Complex Numbers Test 11
Answer Key

1)	B
2)	B
3)	B
4)	B
5)	D
6)	A
7)	D
8)	B
9)	A
10)	A
11)	C
12)	B
13)	A
14)	A
15)	D

Complex Numbers Test 11
Solutions

1. $i^2 = -1$

$= i^0 + i^{31} + i^{10}$

$= 1 + (i^2)^{15} \cdot i + (i^2)^5$

$= 1 + (-1)^{15} \cdot i + (-1)^5$

$= 1 - i - 1$

$= -i$

Correct Answer : B

2. $x^2 + 4x + 5 = 0$ (Use the complete square method to solve equation)

$x^2 + 4x = -5$

$(x + 2)^2 - 4 = -5$

$(x + 2)^2 = -5 + 4$

$(x + 2)^2 = -1 \quad i^2 = -1$

$x + 2 = \pm i$

$x = -2 \pm i$

Correct Answer : B

3. $\left(\dfrac{1+i}{1-i}\right)^{2018}$

$= \left(\dfrac{(1+i)(1+i)}{(1-i)1+i}\right)^{2018}$

$= \left(\dfrac{1+i+i+i^2}{1-i^2}\right)^{2018}$

$= \left(\dfrac{1+2i-1}{1+1}\right)^{2018} = \left(\dfrac{2i}{2}\right)^{2018}$

$= i^{2018}$

$= (i^2)^{1009} = (-1)^{1009} = -1$

Correct Answer : B

4. $\boxed{i^2 = -1}$

$(i^2)^{1009} \cdot i + (i^2)^{1010} + (i^2)^{1010} \cdot i$

$(-1)^{1009} \cdot i + (-1)^{2010} + (-1)^{1010} \cdot i$

$= -i + 1 + i$

$= 1$

Correct Answer : B

5. $a = 1 - 5i$ and $b = 1 + 5i$, then

$a \cdot b = (1 - 5i) \cdot (1 + 5i)$

$= 1 - 25i^2$

$= 1 + 25$

$= 26$

Correct Answer : D

6. $\dfrac{4}{1+i\sqrt{3}} = \dfrac{4}{1+i\sqrt{3}}\left(\dfrac{1-i\sqrt{3}}{1-i\sqrt{3}}\right) \quad i^2 = -1$

$= \dfrac{4 - 4i\sqrt{3}}{1 - 3i^2} = \dfrac{4 - 4i\sqrt{3}}{1 + 3}$

$= \dfrac{4 - 4i\sqrt{3}}{4} = 1 - i\sqrt{3}$

Correct Answer : A

Complex Numbers Test 11
Solutions

7. $\dfrac{a-bi}{a+bi} = \dfrac{(a-bi)(a-bi)}{(a+bi)(a-bi)}$

$= \dfrac{a^2 - abi - bai + b^2i^2}{a^2 - b^2i^2}$

$= \dfrac{a^2 - 2abi - b^2}{a^2 + b^2}$

Correct Answer : D

8. $(i - 2)(i + 6)$

$= i^2 + 6i - 2i - 12$

$= -1 + 4i - 12$

$= -13 + 4i$

Correct Answer : B

9. $\sqrt{-5} \cdot \sqrt{75}$

Rile : $i^2 = -1$

$\sqrt{5i^2} \cdot \sqrt{75}$

$= \sqrt{5 \cdot 75 i^2}$

$= \sqrt{15 \cdot 25 i^2}$

$= 5i\sqrt{15}$

Correct Answer : A

10. $i^2 = -1$

$24 = -4x^2$

$-6 = x^2$

$6i^2 = x^2$

$\pm i\sqrt{6} = x$

Correct Answer : A

11. $\left(\dfrac{1}{2} - \dfrac{i}{2}\right) \cdot \left(\dfrac{1}{2} + \dfrac{i}{2}\right)$

$= \dfrac{1}{4} + \dfrac{i}{4} - \dfrac{i}{4} - \dfrac{i^2}{4}$

$= \dfrac{1}{4} - \dfrac{i^2}{4}$

$= \dfrac{1}{4} + \dfrac{1}{4} = \dfrac{2}{4} = \dfrac{1}{2}$

Correct Answer : C

12. $\sqrt{-5} + \sqrt{-20} + \sqrt{-125}$

$= i\sqrt{5} + 2i\sqrt{5} + 5i\sqrt{5}$

$= 8i\sqrt{5}$

Correct Answer : B

13. $\dfrac{2}{3} - \dfrac{i}{6} = \dfrac{4}{6} - \dfrac{i}{6}$

$= \dfrac{4-i}{6}$

Correct Answer : A

14. $\dfrac{4}{i} + i = \dfrac{4+i^2}{i} = \dfrac{4-1}{i} = \dfrac{3}{i} \cdot \dfrac{i}{i} = \dfrac{3i}{i^2} = \dfrac{3i}{-1} = -3i$

Correct Answer : A

15. $i^{2018} \cdot i^{2019}$

Rule : $i^2 = -1$

$= (i^2)^{1009} \cdot (i^2)^{1009} \cdot i$

$= (-1)^{1009} \cdot (-1)^{1009} \cdot i$

$= (-1) \cdot (-1) \; i$

$= i$

Correct Answer : D

Exponential Growth, Decay & Data Interpretation Test 12

1. An investment of $600 increases at a rate of 4% per year. Find the value of investment after 12 years. (Round your answer to the nearest dollar).

A) $961

B) $984

C) $995

D) $996

E) $1,020

2. In college, next year's tuition will increase by 15% per year. If this year's tuition in college was $660, what will it be next year?

A) $650

B) $688

C) $745

D) $759

E) $81

3. Melissa's monthly electrical bill was $125. Due to a rate decrease, her monthly bill is now $110. To the nearest to tenth of a percent, by what percent did the amount of the customers electrical bill decrease?

A) 8%

B) 10%

C) 12%

D) 15%

E) 18%

4. The following chart show market stock in supermarkets which buy tea, coffee, soda and water after they sell them. Their prices are given in the chart.

	Cost	Sale
Tea	20	25
Coffee	12	18
Soda	20	24
Water	90	120
Hot Chocolate	100	125

Which product has the highest rate of profit?

A) Tea

B) Coffee

C) Soda

D) Water

E) Hot Chocolate

Exponential Growth, Decay & Data Interpretation Test 12

5. In math class, everyone has to do a math project. Out of 24 students, 25% have completed their projects. How many students have completed their projects?

   A) 3 students

   B) 4 students

   C) 5 students

   D) 6 students

   E) 10 students

6. Find the bank account balance if the account starts with $360, has an annual rate of 6%, and the money is left in the account for 5 years. (Round your answer to the nearest whole)

   A) $380

   B) $482

   C) $522

   D) $544

   E) $566

7. Melisa deposits $200 in her saving account with a rate of 6%. The interests compounded yearly. How much money will Melisa have after 8 years? (Round your answer to the nearest whole)

   A) $315

   B) $319

   C) $325

   D) $330

   E) $384

8. Jenny buys a car for $28,000. The value of the car decreases by 6% each year. Estimate the value after 5 years. (Round your answer nearest to whole)

   A) $20,549

   B) $21,549

   C) $22,549

   D) $23,549

   E) $23,689

Exponential Growth, Decay & Data Interpretation Test 12

9. Students were asked whether they spent a long time or a short time to complete their math test. The circle graph shows the responses of 90 students. How many students thought they completed in a short time?

Math test time

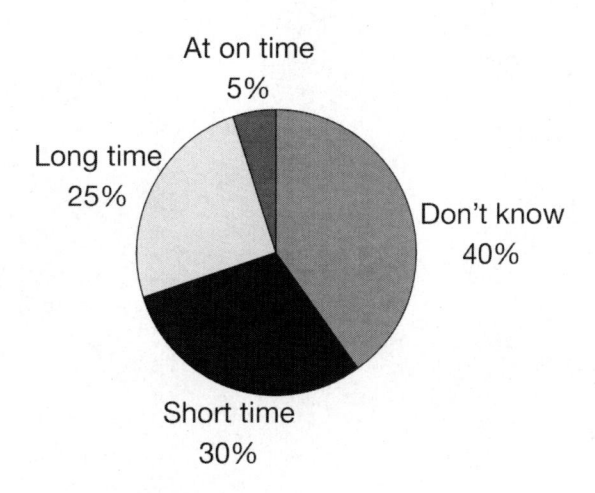

At on time 5%
Long time 25%
Don't know 40%
Short time 30%

A) 3 students

B) 6 students

C) 9 students

D) 27 students

E) 30 students

10. Which of following graphs have no correlation?

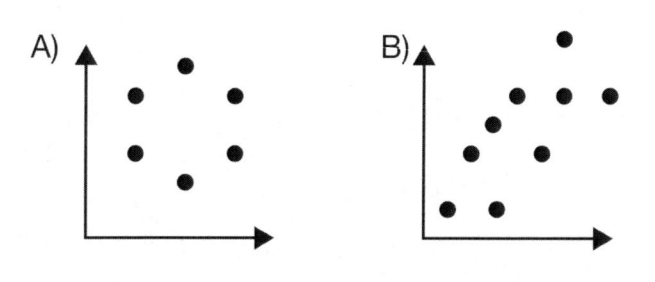

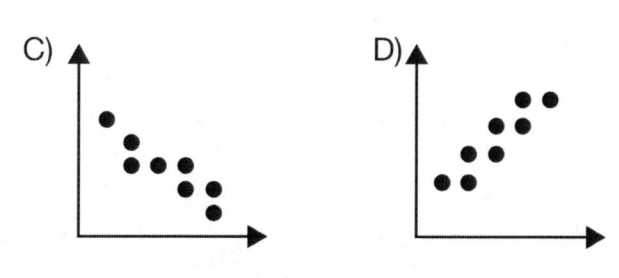

A)

B)

C)

D)

E) None of above

94

Exponential Growth, Decay & Data Interpretation Test 12

Use the graph to answer the question 11 to 12.

Students, Favorite Sports

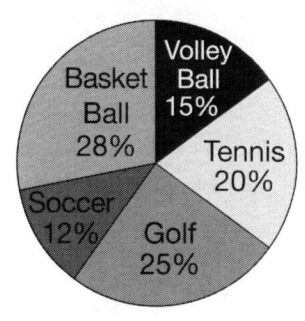

- Basket Ball 28%
- Volley Ball 15%
- Tennis 20%
- Golf 25%
- Soccer 12%

11. Find the number of students who like tennis out of a population of 600 students.

A) 75 students

B) 100 students

C) 120 students

D) 175 students

E) 185 students

12. A circle graph shows the percent of student's favorite sports. Find the number of students who like Volleyball out of a population of 600 students.

A) 75 students

B) 90 students

C) 110 students

D) 120 students

E) 140 students

Exponential Growth, Decay & Data Interpretation Test 12
Answer Key

1)	A
2)	D
3)	C
4)	B
5)	D
6)	B
7)	B
8)	A
9)	D
10)	A
11)	C
12)	B

Exponential Growth, Decay & Data Interpretation Test 12
Solutions

1. $A = P(1 + r)^t$

P = $600

r = 0.04

t = 12 years

$A = P(1 + r)^t$

$A = \$600(1 + 0.04)^{12}$

$A = \$600(1.04)^{12}$

A = $960 . 61...

A = $961

Correct Answer : A

2. Increasing tuition $\$660 \cdot \dfrac{15}{100} = \dfrac{9900}{100} = \$99$

Next year tuition total = $660 + $99 = $759

Correct Answer : D

3. Decrease: $\dfrac{\text{decrease amount}}{\text{original amount}} = \dfrac{\$125 - \$110}{\$125}$

$= \dfrac{15}{125} = \dfrac{3}{25}$

$= \dfrac{3}{25} \cdot \dfrac{4}{4} = \dfrac{12}{100} = 12\%$

Correct Answer : C

4. $\text{Tea} = \dfrac{25-20}{20} = \dfrac{5}{20} = 25\%$

$\text{Coffee} = \dfrac{18-12}{12} = \dfrac{6}{12} = 50\%$

$\text{Soda} = \dfrac{24-20}{20} = \dfrac{4}{20} = 20\%$

$\text{Water} = \dfrac{120-90}{90} = \dfrac{30}{90} \approx 33\%$

$\text{Hot Chocolate} = \dfrac{125-100}{100} = \dfrac{25}{100} = 25\%$

the highest rate of profit is Coffee.

Correct Answer : B

5. $\dfrac{24 \cdot 25}{100} = 6$ students.

Correct Answer : D

6. $A = P(1+r)^t$

P = $360

r = 0.06

t = 5 years

$A = P(1 + r)^t$

$A = \$360(1 + 0.06)^5$

$A = \$360(1.06)^5$

A = $481.76...

A ≈ $482

Correct Answer : B

Exponential Growth, Decay & Data Interpretation Test 12
Solutions

7. $A = P(1+r)^t$

$P = \$200$

$r = 0.06$

$t = 8$ years

$A = P(1 + r)^t$

$A = \$200(1 + 0.06)^8$

$A = \$200(1.06)^8$

$A = \$318.76...$

$A \approx \$319$

Correct Answer : B

8. $A = P(1 - r)^t$

$P = \$28,000$

$r = 0.06$

$t = 5$ years

$A = \$28,000(1 - 0.06)^5$

$A = \$28,000(0.94)^5$

$A = \$20,549$

Correct Answer : A

9. From graph

$x = \dfrac{30 \cdot 90}{100} = 27$

Correct Answer : D

10. No Correlation

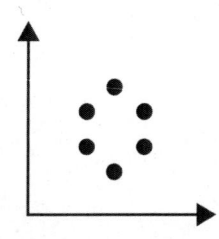

Correct Answer : A

11. Students who like tennis $= \dfrac{20 \cdot 600}{100} = 120$

Correct Answer : C

12. Students who like Volleyball $= \dfrac{15 \cdot 600}{100} = 90$

Correct Answer : B

Sequences & Transformations of Functions Test 13

1. $1, \frac{1}{2}, 0, -\frac{1}{2}, -1,$?

What is the missing value of in this sequence?

A) $\frac{1}{2}$

B) $\frac{1}{4}$

C) $-\frac{1}{2}$

D) $-\frac{1}{4}$

E) $-\frac{1}{8}$

2. Which of following is arithmetic sequence?

A) 2, 4, 6, 7, 12, 18,...

B) 3, 6, 12, 24,...

C) 5, 10, 15, 20, 25,...

D) 0, 1, 3, 4, 7,...

E) None of above

3. Which of following is geometric sequence?

A) 3, 6, 9, 8, 12,...

B) 3, 6, 12, 24,...

C) 4, 8, 12, 16,...

D) 1, 3, 5, 7,...

E) None of above

4.   –6, 0, 6, 12, 18,...

What is the 15th term of this sequence?

A) 36

B) 48

C) 56

D) 78

E) 84

5. If $a_n = 2^n - 1$, then what is the 4th term of this sequence?

A) 4

B) 8

C) 12

D) 15

E) 18

Sequences & Transformations of Functions Test 13

6. What is the sum of the even integers between 35 to 75?

A) 1,925
B) 2,925
C) 3,850
D) 4,850
E) 3,980

7. The operation sequence is given below and it has a rule.

$$3 \otimes 4 = 22$$
$$5 \otimes 2 = 20$$
$$7 \otimes 8 = 66$$

What is solution of $6 \otimes 7 = ?$

A) 40
B) 44
C) 50
D) 52
E) 56

8. $\oplus$ Is a operation in the set of positive integer and following is given

$$x \oplus y = \begin{cases} \dfrac{x+y}{2}, & \text{if } x+y = \text{even} \\ \dfrac{x+y+1}{2}, & \text{if } x+y = \text{old} \end{cases}$$

What is the solution of $3 \oplus (5 \oplus 4) = ?$

A) 3
B) 4
C) 5
D) 6
E) 8

9. What is the coordinate of the vertices of (–2, –4) when the vertices reflection across the y–axis.

A) (–2, –4)
B) (2, –4)
C) (2, 4)
D) (–2, 4)
E) (0, –4)

100

Sequences & Transformations of Functions Test 13

10. If $f(x) = x^2 + 3$ which of following is the graph of $g(x) = f(x - 3)$.

A)

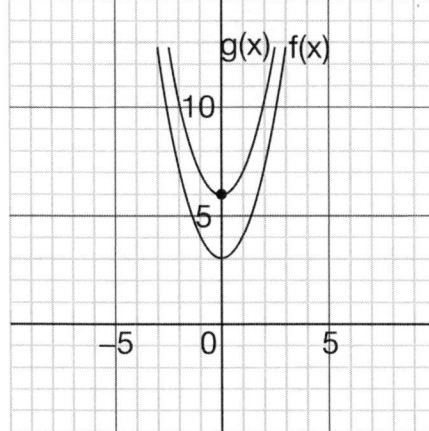

B)

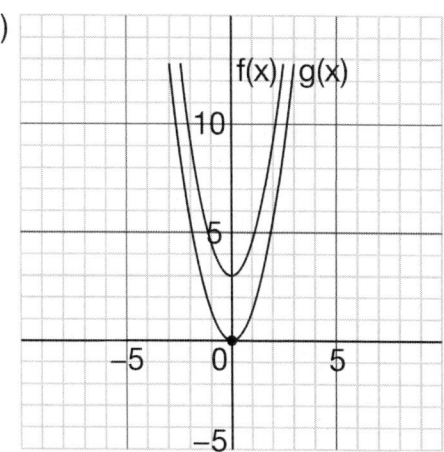

C)

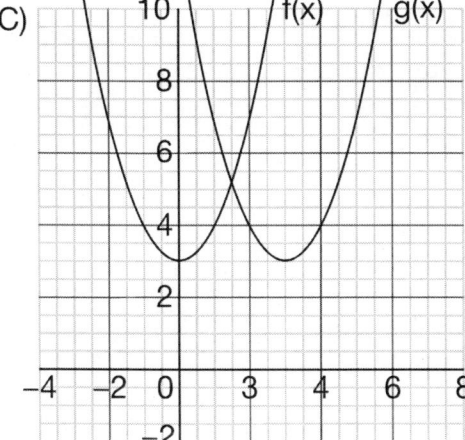

D)

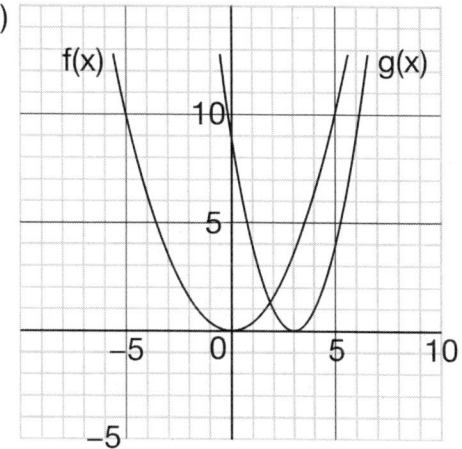

E)

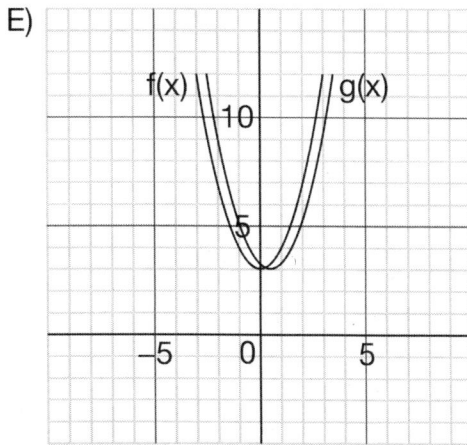

101

Sequences & Transformations of Functions Test 13

11. Given the graph of the parent function is $f(x) = x^2 + 4$

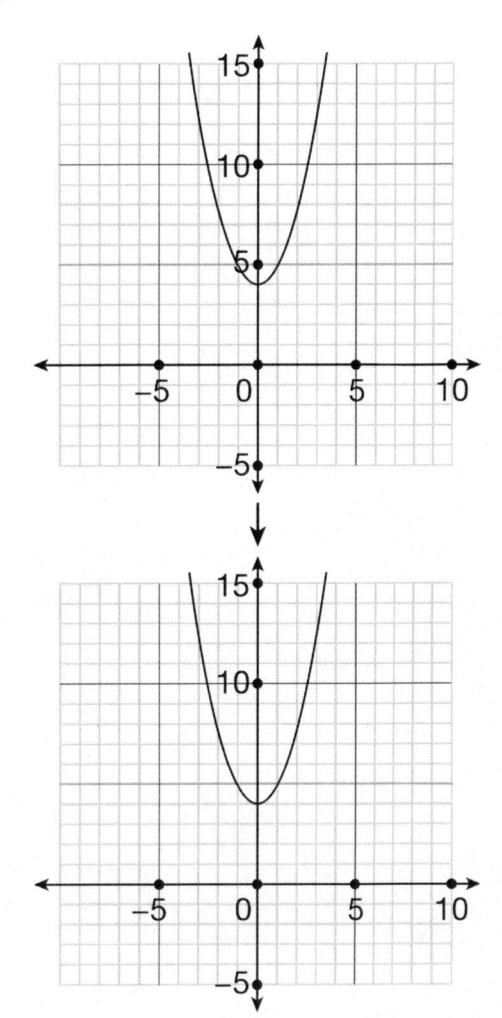

Which function below correctly describes the graph of g(x)?

A) $g(x) = (x - 4)^2 + 3$

B) $g(x) = (x - 4)^2 - 3$

C) $g(x) = (x + 4)^2 + 3$

D) $g(x) = x^2 + 3$

E) $g(x) = x^2 + 4$

12. Describe how the graph of $f(x) = x^2$ can be transformed to the graph of the given function of

$$g(x) = (x + 3)^2 + 2.$$

A) Shift the graph of $f(x) = x^2$ right 3 units and then up 2 units.

B) Shift the graph of $f(x) = x^2$ right 3 units and then down 2 units.

C) Shift the graph of $f(x) = x^2$ left 3 units and then up 2 units.

D) Shift the graph of $f(x) = x^2$ left 3 units and then down 2 units.

E) Shift the graph of $f(x) = x^2$ right 2 units and then up 3 units.

Sequences & Transformations of Functions Test 13

13. Given the graph of the parent function below which of following is match the equation to its parent function?

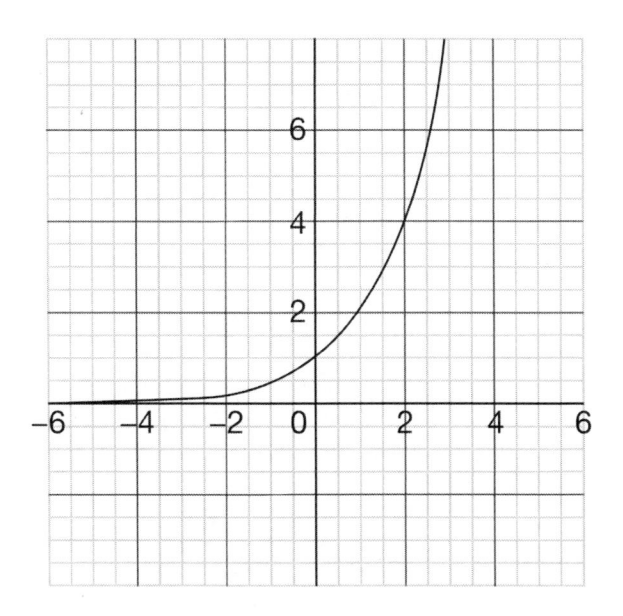

A) $y = 2x$

B) $y = 2^x$

C) $y = 2^{x+2}$

D) $y = -2^x$

E) $y = \left(\frac{1}{2}x\right)^2$

14. Point M is plotted in the graph below.

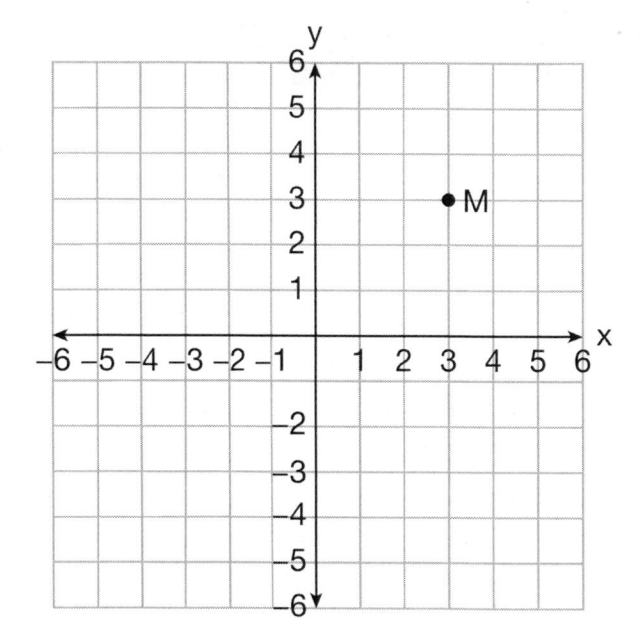

What would be the location of the image of M after it is reflected over the x-axis?

A) $M^I = (0, 3)$

B) $M^I = (3, 0)$

C) $M^I = (-3, 3)$

D) $M^I = (-3, -3)$

E) $M^I = (3, -3)$

103

Sequences & Transformations of Functions Test 13

15. The operation sequence is given below and it has a rule.

$$3 \otimes 4 = 22$$
$$5 \otimes 2 = 20$$
$$7 \otimes 8 = 66$$

What is the solution of $6 \otimes 7$?

A) 40

B) 44

C) 50

D) 52

E) 58

16. Φ and ⊕ are functions on real numbers.

$x \, \Phi \, y = \dfrac{x^2 + y}{4}$ and $x \oplus y = \dfrac{3xy}{5}$

$(2 \, \Phi \, 1) \oplus (3 \, \Phi \, 1) = ?$

A) $\dfrac{25}{4}$

B) $\dfrac{27}{4}$

C) $\dfrac{15}{8}$

D) $\dfrac{17}{2}$

E) $\dfrac{17}{3}$

Sequences & Transformations of Functions Test 13
Answer Key

1)	C
2)	C
3)	B
4)	D
5)	D
6)	A
7)	D
8)	B
9)	B
10)	C
11)	A
12)	A
13)	A
14)	E
15)	D
16)	C

Sequences &Transformations of Functions Test 13
Solutions

1. The common difference is: $\frac{1}{2} - 1 = -\frac{1}{2}$

   Correct Answer : C

2. Since arithmetic sequence means common difference, then only choice C can be correct. 5, 10, 15, 20, 25 ...
   +5 +5 +5 +5

   Correct Answer : C

3. Since geometric sequence means common ratio, then only choice B has common ratio. 3, 6, 12, 24 $\Rightarrow \frac{6}{3} = \frac{12}{6} = \frac{24}{12}$

   Correct Answer : B

4. $a_n = a_1 + (n-1)d$
   $a_{15} = -6 + (15-1) \cdot 6$
   $a_{15} = -6 + (14) \cdot 6$
   $a_{15} = -6 + 84$
   $a_{15} = 78$

   Correct Answer : D

5. Since $a_n = 2^n - 1$, then 4th term
   $a_4 = 2^4 - 1$
   $a_4 = 16 - 1$
   $a_4 = 15$

   Correct Answer : D

6. Arithmetic sequence: 36, 38, 40,...74
   $d = 2$
   $n = 35$
   $S_n \frac{35(36+74)}{2}$
   $= \frac{35 \cdot 110}{2} = \frac{3850}{2} = 1,925$

   Correct Answer : A

7. The rule of the operation is
   $x \otimes y = x \cdot y + 10$
   Check
   $3 \otimes 4 = 3 \cdot 4 + 10 = 22$
   $5 \otimes 2 = 5 \cdot 2 + 10 = 20$
   $7 \otimes 8 = 7 \cdot 8 + 10 = 66$
   so
   $6 \otimes 7 = 6 \cdot 7 + 10 = 52$

   Correct Answer : D

8. $5 \oplus 4 = 5 + 4 =$ odd then $\frac{5+4+1}{2} = 5$ and
   $3 \oplus 5 = 3 + 5 =$ even then $\frac{5+3}{2} = 4$

   Correct Answer : B

Sequences & Transformations of Functions Test 13
Solutions

9. Reflection across the y–axis means keep same y–axis and change sign of x–axis.

(–2, –4) → reflection across the y–axis is (2, –4)

Correct Answer : B

10. $f(x) = x^2 + 3$ and $g(x) = f(x - 3)$

Graph of both functions are:

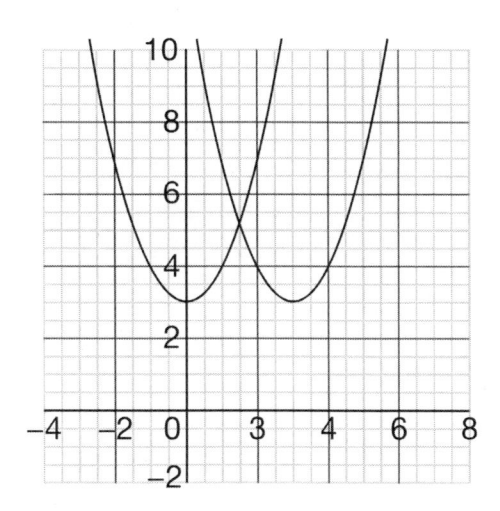

Correct Answer : C

11. From the all choices only choice A can be correct.

Correct Answer : A

12. From the all choices only choice A can be correct.

Correct Answer : A

13. From the graph only choice B can be correct.

Correct Answer : A

14. Point M (3, 3) reflected over the x–axis M' = (3, –3)

Correct Answer : E

15. The rule of the operation is

$x \otimes y = x \cdot y + 10$

Check

$3 \otimes 4 = 3 \cdot 4 + 10 = 22$

$5 \otimes 2 = 5 \cdot 2 + 10 = 20$

$7 \otimes 8 = 7 \cdot 8 + 10 = 66$

Then

$6 \otimes 7 = 6 \cdot 7 + 10 = 52$

Correct Answer : D

16. $(2 \Phi 1) = \dfrac{2^2 + 1}{4} = \dfrac{5}{4}$

$(3 \Phi 1) = \dfrac{3^2 + 1}{4} = \dfrac{10}{4}$

$\left(\dfrac{5}{4} \oplus \dfrac{10}{4}\right) = \dfrac{3 \cdot \dfrac{5}{4} \cdot \dfrac{10}{4}}{5} = \dfrac{150}{80} = \dfrac{150}{80} = \dfrac{15}{8}$

Correct Answer : C

Permutation and Combination Test 14

1. Evaluate $_7P_4 = ?$

   A) 980
   B) 1200
   C) 1,120
   D) 1,200
   E) 1,320

2. The science quiz consists of 5 questions, which must be answered within each permitting a choice of 3 alternatives. In how many ways may a student fill in the answers if they answer each question?

   A) 3
   B) 9
   C) 81
   D) 243
   E) 726

3. In how many ways may can six students line up to get on a class?

   A) 120
   B) 240
   C) 360
   D) 460
   E) 720

4. How many distinct permutations of the word "mathematicians" begin and end with the letter "a"?

   A) 268
   B) 364
   C) 476
   D) 540
   E) 560

5. How many 4–element subsets are in the set M = {4, 8, 12, 16, 20, 24, 28}?

   A) 10
   B) 15
   C) 20
   D) 25
   E) 35

6. A jar contains 8 blue and 7 red marbles. How many ways 4 blue and 3 red marbles be chosen?

   A) 2,240
   B) 2,550
   C) 2,850
   D) 3,000
   E) 3,450

Permutation and Combination Test 14

7. A{0, 1, 2, 3, 4, 5, 6, 7, 8, 9}

What is the probability of the selecting an odd number in the set A?

A) $\dfrac{1}{2}$

B) $\dfrac{1}{3}$

C) $\dfrac{1}{4}$

D) $\dfrac{1}{5}$

E) $\dfrac{1}{8}$

8. Let D, L and M be sets.

D = {a, b, c, d, e}

L = {b, c, e, q, r}

M = D∩L is given. According to these sets which of the following is equal to set L∪(D∩M)?

A) D

B) L

C) M∪D

D) L∪D

E) L∪M

9. Let A and B be two sets.

A = {−7, −6, −5, −4, −3, −2, −1, 0, 1, 2, 3, 4, 5, 6}

B = {−9, −7, −5, −3, −1, 3, 5, 7, 9}

Which of the following is the given set of s(A∩B)?

A) (−9, −5, −3, −1, 0, 1, 3, 5)

B) (−7, −5, −3, −1, 3, 5)

C) (−9, −7, −5, −3, −1, 3, 5, 6)

D) (−7, −5, −3, −1, 1, 2, 3, 4, 5)

E) (−7, −5, −3, −1, 3, 5, 6)

Permutation and Combination Test 14
Answer Key

1)	C
2)	D
3)	E
4)	B
5)	E
6)	A
7)	A
8)	B
9)	B

Permutation and Combination Test 14
Solutions

1. $P(n, r) = \dfrac{n!}{(n-r)!}$

    $P_{8,4} = \dfrac{7!}{7-4!} = \dfrac{7 \cdot 6 \cdot 5 \cdot 4 \cdot 3!}{3!} = 7 \cdot 6 \cdot 5 \cdot 4 = 1,120$

    Correct Answer : C

2. $3^5 = 3 \cdot 3 \cdot 3 \cdot 3 \cdot 3 = 243$

    Correct Answer : D

3. $6! = 6 \cdot 5 \cdot 4 \cdot 3 \cdot 2 \cdot 1 = 720$

    Correct Answer : E

4. $\dfrac{14!}{(14-3)! \cdot 3!} = \dfrac{14 \cdot 13 \cdot 12 \cdot 11!}{(11)! \cdot 3!} = \dfrac{14 \cdot 13 \cdot \cancel{12}^{2}}{\cancel{3 \cdot 2}}$

    $= 14 \cdot 13 \cdot 2 = 364$

    Correct Answer : B

5. We choose 4 elements from a set of 7 elements.

    $\dfrac{7!}{(7-4)! \cdot 4!} = \dfrac{7!}{(3)! \cdot 4!} = \dfrac{7 \cdot 6 \cdot 5 \cdot \cancel{4!}}{3! \cdot \cancel{4!}}$

    $= \dfrac{7 \cdot \cancel{6} \cdot 5}{\cancel{3 \cdot 2}} = 7 \cdot 5 = 35$

    Correct Answer : E

6. $C(n, r) = \dfrac{n!}{r!(n-r)!}$

    $C_{8,4} = \dfrac{8!}{4!(8-4)!} = \dfrac{8!}{4! \cdot (4)!} = \dfrac{8 \cdot 7 \cdot 6 \cdot 5 \cdot \cancel{4!}}{\cancel{4!} \cdot 4!}$

    $= \dfrac{8 \cdot 7 \cdot 6 \cdot 5}{4 \cdot 3 \cdot 2 \cdot 1} = 70$

    $C_{7,3} = \dfrac{7!}{3!(7-3)!} = \dfrac{7!}{3! \cdot (4)!} = \dfrac{7 \cdot 6 \cdot 5 \cdot \cancel{4!}}{3! \cdot \cancel{4!}}$

    $= \dfrac{7 \cdot 6 \cdot 5}{3 \cdot 2 \cdot 1} = 35$

    $35 \cdot 70 = 2,450$

    Correct Answer : A

7. Probability of the selected odd:

    $= \dfrac{P \text{ odd numbers}}{\text{total}}$

    $= \dfrac{5}{10} = \dfrac{1}{2}$

    Correct Answer : A

8. $M = D \cap L = \{b, c, e\}$ then $D \cap M = \{b, c, e\}$

    So; $L \cup (D \cap M) = \{b, c, e, q, r\} \cup \{b, c, e\} = L$

    Correct Answer : B

9. $A = \{-7, -6, -5, -4, -3, -2, -1, 0, 1, 2, 3, 4, 5, 6\}$

    $B = \{-9, -7, -5, -3, -1, 3, 5, 7, 9\}$

    $s(A \cap B) = \{-7, -5, -3, -1, 3, 5\}$

    Correct Answer : B

Mixed Review Test III

1.
$$x + 3ky = 12$$
$$5x - 12y = 18$$

In the system of equations above, k is a constant. For what value of k will the system of equations have no solutions?

A) $-\dfrac{4}{5}$

B) $\dfrac{4}{5}$

C) $\dfrac{5}{4}$

D) $-\dfrac{5}{4}$

E) $-\dfrac{3}{8}$

2. In the polynomial below, a is the constant. If the polynomial P(x) is divisible by x+2 then find the value of a.
$$P(x) = 2x^3 + ax^2 - x + 2$$

A) 2

B) 3

C) 5

D) 7

E) 9

3. $i^{2019} + i^{2020} + i^{2021}$

Which of the following is equivalent to the complex number shown above?

A) i

B) 1

C) 2i

D) 2

E) –i

4. An investment of $600 increases at a rate of 4% per year. Find the value of investment after 12 years. (Round your answer to the nearest dollar).

A) $941

B) $951

C) $961

D) $992

E) $993

5. If $P(x-2) = x^2 + 2x + 1$, then find $P(x + 1)$?

A) $x^2 + 8x + 16$

B) $-x^2 + 8x + 16$

C) $x^2 - 8x + 16$

D) $x^2 + 8x - 16$

E) $x^2 + 8x + 12$

112

Mixed Review Test III

6. $A = 3x + 1 = 4y + 2 = 5z + 3$

From the above equations x, y, and z are positive integer and A is a two digit number. What is the smallest value of A?

A) 58
B) 68
C) 78
D) 88
E) 98

7. Melisa makes an online purchase SAT book and 25% discount is applied to the book price, then 4% tax is added to this discounted price. Which of the following represents the amount Melisa pays for an item with a book price in d dollars?

A) 0.75d
B) 0.78d
C) 0.88d
D) 0.92d
E) 0.99d

8. $\triangle = x^2 - 2x + 1$
$\bigcirc = x^2 - 1$

From above, if $\bigcirc = \triangle$, then find x.

A) 1
B) 2
C) 3
D) 4
E) 6

9.

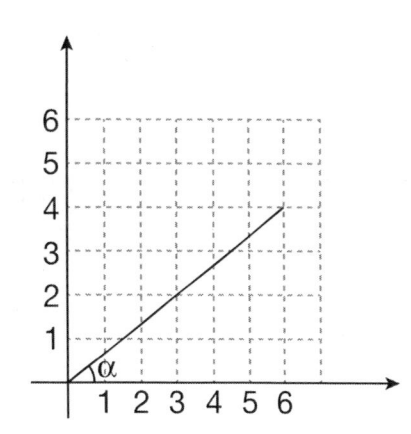

What is the equation of the function?

A) $y = 2x$
B) $y = \dfrac{2}{3}x$
C) $y = x + 7$
D) $y = 2x + 3$
E) $y = 2x + 5$

Mixed Review Test III

10. $\frac{1}{a} = \frac{1}{b} + \frac{1}{c}$ Find b in terms of a and c.

A) $b = \frac{ac}{c-a}$

B) $b = \frac{ac}{a-c}$

C) $b = ac$

D) $b = \frac{1}{c-a}$

E) $b = \frac{1}{a-c}$

11. If $\frac{x}{y} = \frac{a}{b} = \frac{2}{3}$ and $y^2 - b^2 = 27$, then what is the value of $x^2 - a^2$?

A) 12

B) 20

C) 24

D) 25

E) 30

12. If $a = 1 - 5i$ and $b = 1 + 5i$, then which of the following is equal to $a \cdot b$?

A) 10

B) 15

C) 25

D) 26

E) 28

13. The price of a book has been discounted 20%. The sale price is $60. What is the original price?

A) $25

B) $45

C) $65

D) $75

E) $80

114

Mixed Review Test III
Answer Key

1)	A
2)	B
3)	B
4)	C
5)	A
6)	A
7)	B
8)	A
9)	B
10)	A
11)	A
12)	D
13)	D

Mixed Review Test III
Solutions

1. $x + 3ky = 12$

$5x - 12y = 18$

$m_1 = \dfrac{-1}{3k}$, $m_2 = \dfrac{+5}{12}$

if a system has no solution, slopes are equal

$m_1 = m_2$

$\dfrac{-1}{3k} = \dfrac{+5}{12}$, $15k = -12$

$k = \dfrac{-12}{15} = \dfrac{-4}{5}$

Correct Answer : A

2. $P(x+2) = 0$, $x+2 = 0$, $x = -2$

$P(-2) = 2(-2)^3 + a(-2)^2 - (-2) + 2$

$P(-2) = -16 + 4a + 2 + 2$

$0 = -16 + 4a + 4$

$0 = -12 + 4a$

$12 = 4a$

$3 = a$

Correct Answer : B

3. $\boxed{i^2 = -1}$

$(i^2)^{1009} \cdot i + (i^2)^{1010} + (i^2)^{1010} \cdot i$

$(-1)^{1009} \cdot i + (-1)^{2010} + (-1)^{1010} \cdot i$

$= \cancel{-i} + 1 + \cancel{i}$

$= 1$

Correct Answer : B

4. $A = P(1 + r)^t$

$P = \$600$

$r = 0.04$

$t = 12$ years

$A = P(1 + r)^t$

$A = \$600(1 + 0.04)^{12}$

$A = \$600(1.04)^{12}$

$A = \$960 . 61...$

$A = \$961$

Correct Answer : C

5. $P(x - 2) = x^2 + 2x + 1$

To find $P(x + 1)$ plug in $x + 3$ for x in $P(x - 2)$.

$P(x + 3 - 2) = (x + 3)^2 + 2(x + 3) + 1$

$P(x + 1) = x^2 + 6x + 9 + 2x + 6 + 1$

$P(x + 1) = x^2 + 8x + 16$

Correct Answer : A

6. If $A = 3x + 1 = 4y + 2 = 5z + 3$,

then $A + 2 = 3x + 3 = 4y + 4 = 5z + 5$.

$A + 2 = 3(x + 1) = 4(y + 1) = 5(z + 1)$

$A + 2 = \text{LCM}(3, 4, 5) = 60$.

$A + 2 = 60$, then $A = 58$

Correct Answer : A

7. If d represents the price of the book, then $d - 0.25\,d = 0.75d$ (the price of book after the discount)

If a 4% tax is added, the final price $0.75d + 0.04(0.75\,d) = 0.78d$

Correct Answer : B

116

Mixed Review Test III
Solutions

8. If $\bigcirc = \triangle$, then
$$x^2 - 2x + 1 = x^2 - 1$$
$$-2x + 1 = -1$$
$$-2x = -2$$
$$x = 1$$

Correct Answer : A

9. $\tan\alpha = \frac{2}{3}$

$(0, 0)$ is satisfied;

$$y - 0 = \frac{2}{3}(x - 0)$$

$$y = \frac{2}{3}x$$

Correct Answer : B

10. $\frac{1}{a} = \frac{1}{b} + \frac{1}{c}$

$\frac{1}{a} = \frac{c+b}{bc}$ (cross multiply)

$ac + ab = bc$

$ac = bc - ab$

$ac = b(c - a)$

$\frac{ac}{c-a} = b$

Correct Answer : A

11. $\frac{x^2}{y^2} = \frac{a^2}{b^2} = \frac{4}{9}$ (Cross multiply)

$9x^2 = 4y^2 \longrightarrow y^2 = \frac{9x^2}{4}$

$9a^2 = 4b^2 \longrightarrow b^2 = \frac{9}{4}a^2$

if $y^2 - b^2 = 27$

$\frac{9x^2}{4} - \frac{9}{4}a^2 = 27$

$\frac{9x^2 - 9a^2}{4} = 27$

$\frac{9(x^2 - a^2)}{4} = 27$

$x^2 - a^2 = \frac{27 \cdot 4}{9} = 12$

Correct Answer : A

12. $a = 1 - 5i$ and $b = 1 + 5i$, then
$$a \cdot b = (1 - 5i) \cdot (1 + 5i)$$
$$= 1 - 25i^2$$
$$= 1 + 25$$
$$= 26$$

Correct Answer : D

13. Original price = $100x$.

20% discount from original price

$= \frac{20 \cdot 100x}{100} = 20x$.

Sales price = $100x - 20x = \$60$

$80x = \$60$

$x = \frac{60}{80} = \frac{6}{8} = \frac{3}{4}$.

Original price $= 100x = 100 \cdot \frac{3}{4} = \frac{300}{4} = 75$.

Correct Answer : D

CHAPTER IV GEOMETRY
Angles & Triangles Test 15

1.

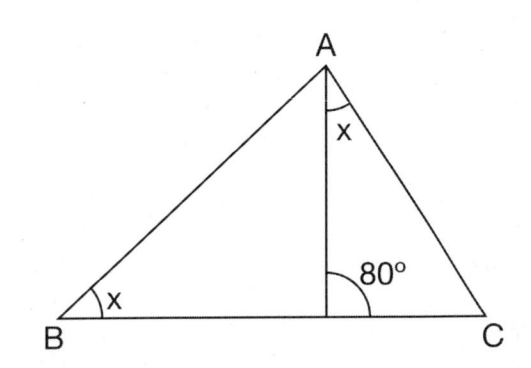

Find the angle of △(BAC) = ?

A) 60°
B) 70°
C) 80°
D) 90°
E) 95°

2.

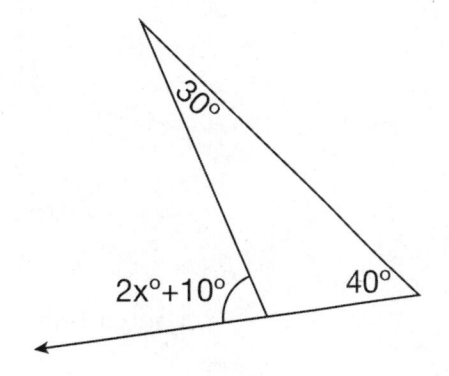

What is the value of x?

A) 10°
B) 20°
C) 30°
D) 40°
E) 45°

3.

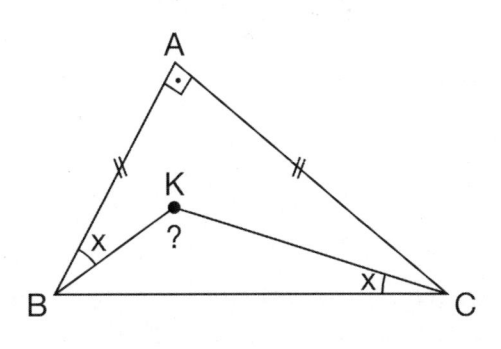

Find the angle of △(BKC) = ?

A) 110°
B) 115°
C) 135°
D) 120°
E) 125°

4. Find the value of x in the diagram.

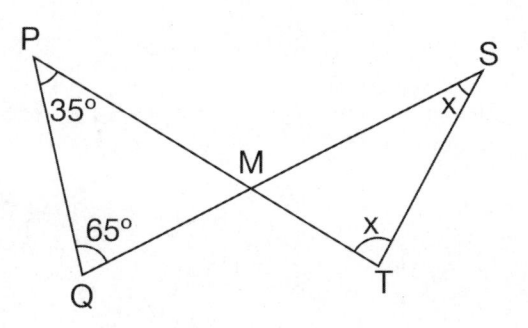

A) 25°
B) 35°
C) 45°
D) 50°
E) 55°

CHAPTER IV GEOMETRY
Angles & Triangles Test 15

5. Find the value of x in the diagram.

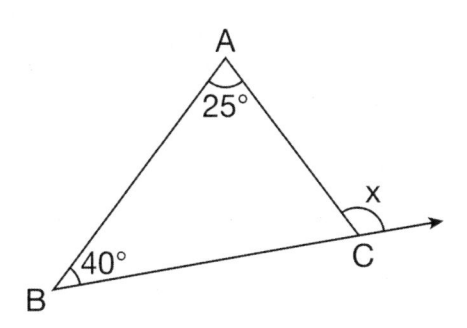

A) 40°
B) 55°
C) 65°
D) 75°
E) 85°

6.

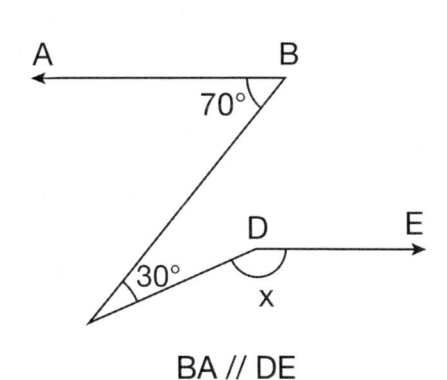

BA // DE

What is the value of x?

A) 120°
B) 140°
C) 150°
D) 160°
E) 175°

7.

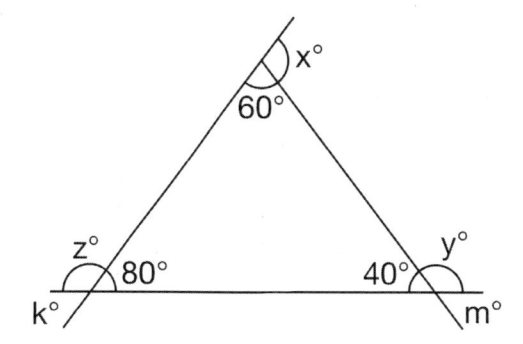

In the figure above, which of the following angles is the greatest?

A) x°
B) y°
C) z°
D) k°
E) m°

8.

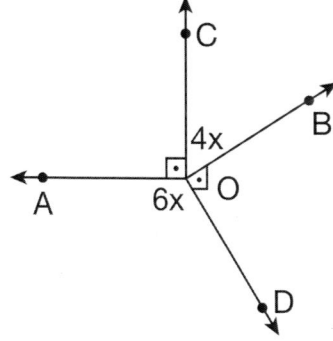

From the figure ∠(BOC) = 6x, ∠(AOD) = 4x, what is the value of x?

A) 10°
B) 18°
C) 30°
D) 40°
E) 45°

CHAPTER IV GEOMETRY
Angles & Triangles Test 15

9.

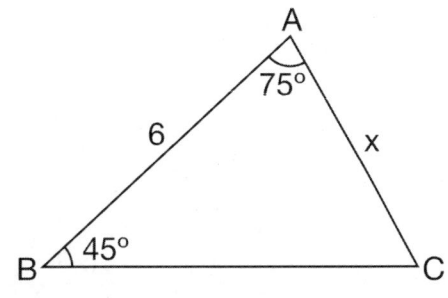

What is the value of x?

A) $\sqrt{6}$

B) $3\sqrt{2}$

C) $2\sqrt{6}$

D) 6

E) 8

10.

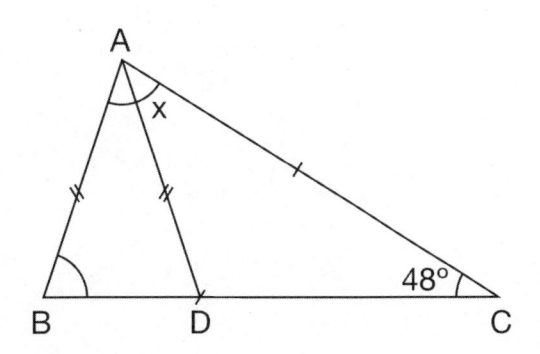

From the following figure, if AB = AD and BC = AC, then what is the value of x?

A) 9°

B) 18°

C) 27°

D) 36°

E) 40°

11.

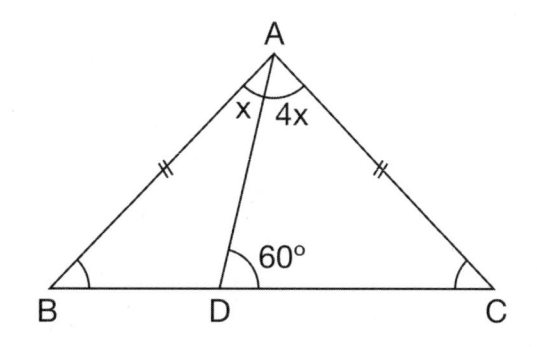

What is the value of x?

A) 10°

B) 20°

C) 30°

D) 40°

E) 50°

12.

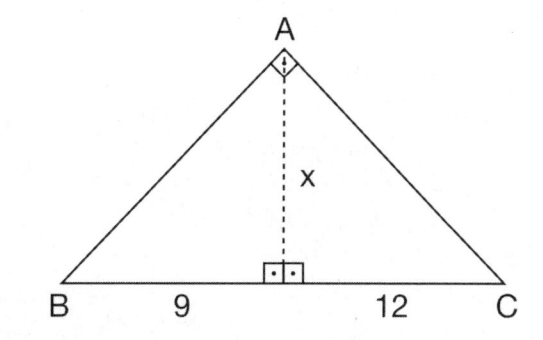

What is the value of x?

A) $3\sqrt{3}$

B) $6\sqrt{3}$

C) $8\sqrt{3}$

D) $12\sqrt{3}$

E) $15\sqrt{3}$

120

Angles & Triangles Test 15
Answer Key

1)	C
2)	C
3)	C
4)	D
5)	C
6)	B
7)	B
8)	B
9)	C
10)	B
11)	B
12)	B

Angles & Triangles Test 15
Solutions

1.

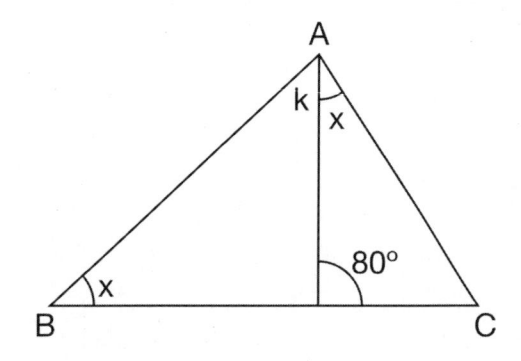

$80° = x + k$

Angle of △(BAC) = $x + k = 80°$

Correct Answer : C

2.

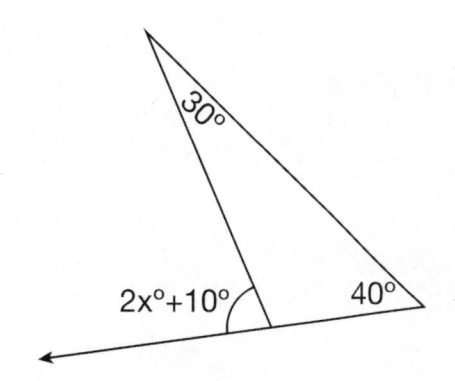

$2x + 10° = 40° + 30°$
$2x = 70° - 10°$
$2x = 60°$
$x = 30°$

Correct Answer : C

3.

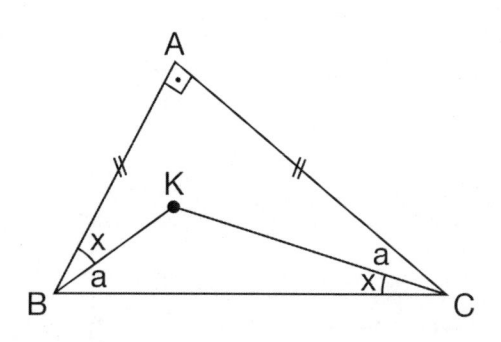

$2x + 2a + 90° = 190°$
$x + a = 45°$
$m(k) + x + a = 180°$
$m(k) + 45° = 180°$
$m(k) = 135°$

Correct Answer : C

4.

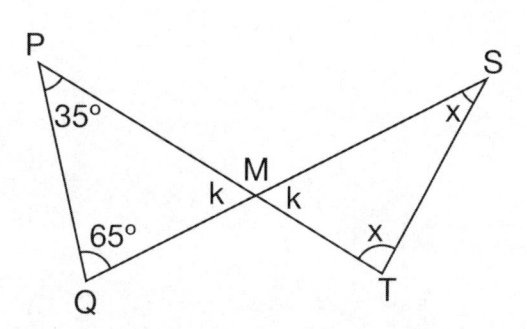

$k + 65° + 35° = 180°$
$k + 100° = 180°$
$k = 180°$
$2x + k = 180°$
$2x + 80° = 180°$
$2x = 10°$
$x = 50°$

Correct Answer : D

Angles & Triangles Test 15
Solutions

5.

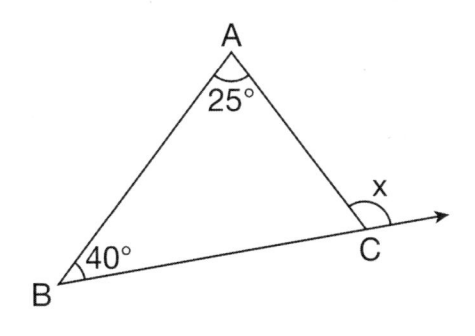

x = 40° + 25°
x = 65°

Correct Answer : C

6.

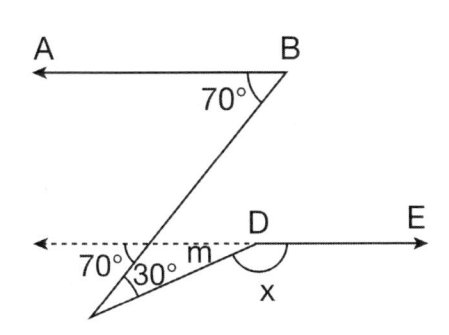

m + 30° = 70°   m = 40°
m + x = 180°
40° + x = 180°   x = 140°

Correct Answer : B

7.

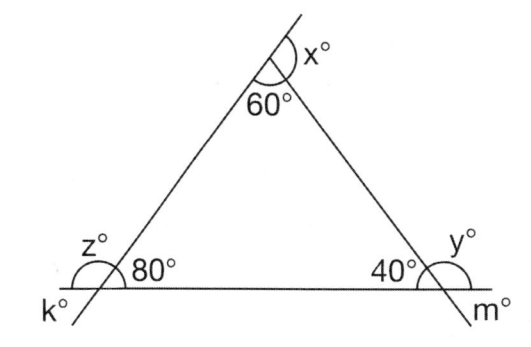

x = 120°
y = 140°
z = 100°
k = 80°
m = 40°

Correct Answer : B

8.

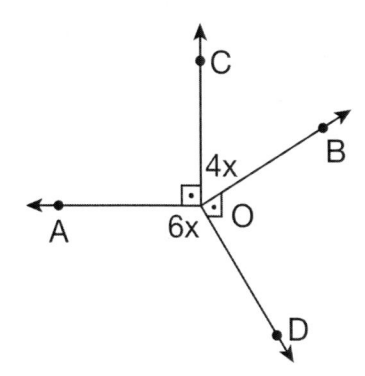

4x + 6x + 90° + 90° = 360°
10x + 180° = 260°
x = 18°

Correct Answer : B

123

Angles & Triangles Test 15
Solutions

9.

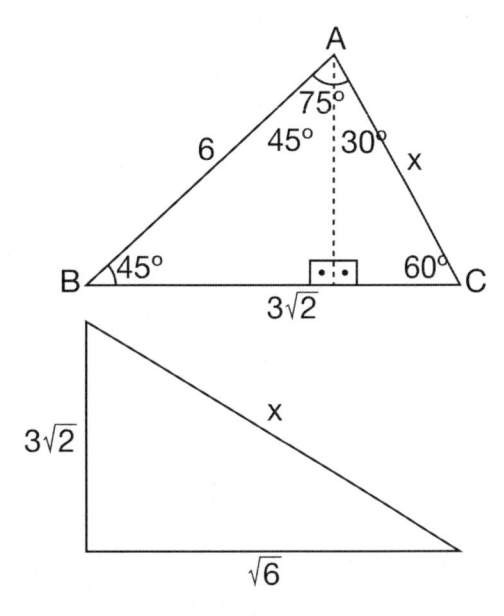

$x^2 = (3\sqrt{2})^2 + (\sqrt{6})^2$

$x^2 = 18 + 6$

$x^2 = 24$

$x = 2\sqrt{6}$

Correct Answer : C

10.

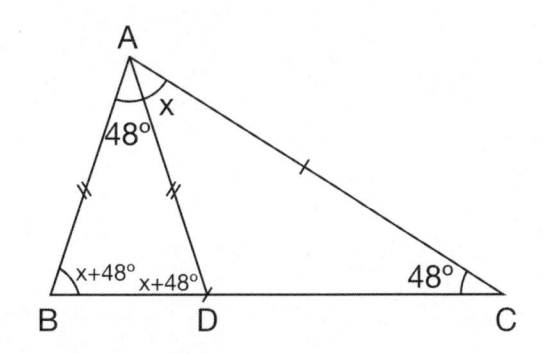

$2x + 144° = 180°$

$x = 18°$

Correct Answer : B

11.

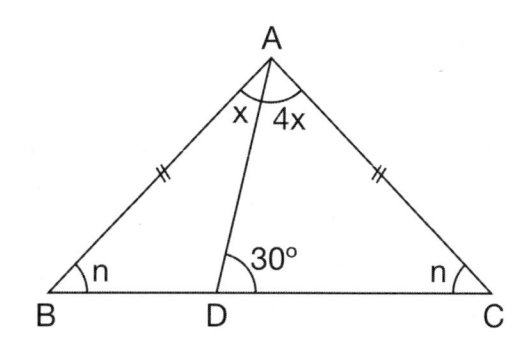

$x + n = 60°$

$5x + 2n = 180°$ $x = 20°$

Correct Answer : B

12.

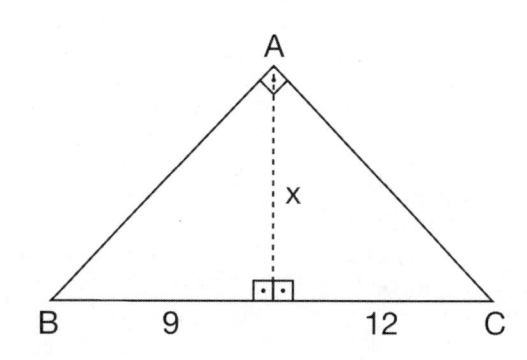

$x^2 = 9 \cdot 12$, $x = \sqrt{9 \cdot 12}$

$x = 6\sqrt{3}$

Correct Answer : B

124

Area & Perimeter Test 16

1. What is the area of an equilateral triangle with a side of 4?

A) $\sqrt{3}$

B) $2\sqrt{3}$

C) $4\sqrt{3}$

D) $6\sqrt{3}$

D) $8\sqrt{3}$

2.

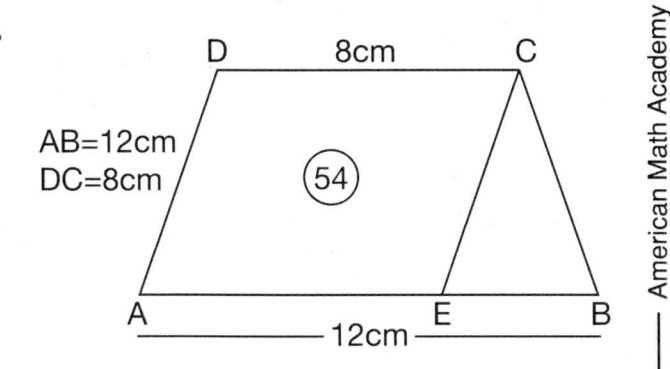

In the above figure, ABCD is a trapezoid and AECD is parallelogram.
AB=12cm, DC=8cm

In the area A(AECD) = 54 cm² then what is the area of triangle CBE?

A) 7.5 cm²

B) 13.5 cm²

C) 27 cm²

D) 54 cm²

E) 72 cm²

3. Which of the following could not be third side of the triangle if a triangle has sides of lengths 4 and 10?

A) 7

B) 8

C) 10

D) 12

E) 14

4.

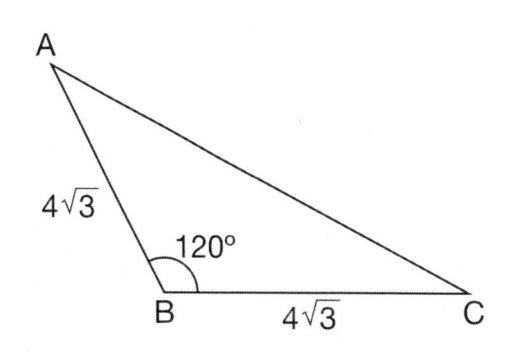

From the figure, what is the area of △(ABC)?

A) $12\sqrt{3}$

B) $8\sqrt{3}$

C) $9\sqrt{3}$

D) $18\sqrt{3}$

E) $20\sqrt{3}$

Area & Perimeter Test 16

5. In the figure below, O is the center of the circle. If OB = AO = 10cm and BC = 12cm, what is the area of A(ACB)?

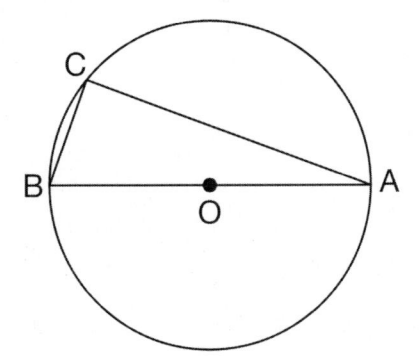

A) 24

B) 48

C) 64

D) 96

E) 104

6.

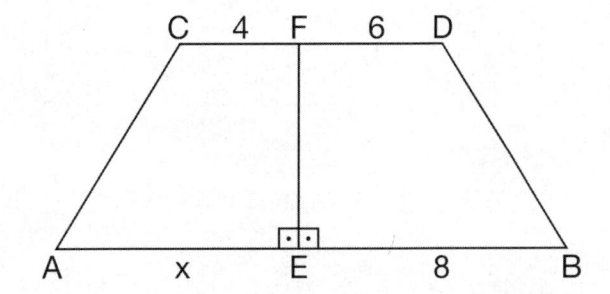

In the above figure, if the area of AEFC is equal to the area of EBDF, what is the value of x?

A) 6

B) 8

C) 10

D) 12

E) 15

7. The angles of a triangle are in the ratio of 4 : 5 : 9. What is the degree measure of the smallest angle

A) 40°

B) 30°

C) 25°

D) 20°

E) 35°

8. What is the area of the triangle below?

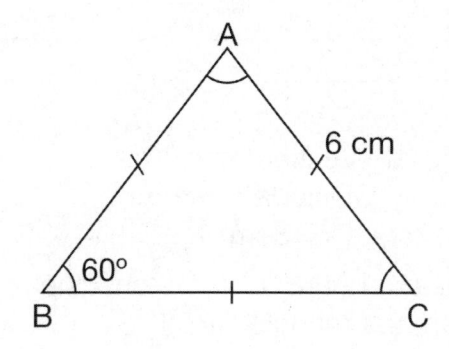

A) $3\sqrt{3}$

B) $6\sqrt{3}$

C) $9\sqrt{3}$

D) $12\sqrt{3}$

E) $15\sqrt{3}$

Area & Perimeter Test 16

9. What is the area of the following square if the length of AC is $2\sqrt{2}$?

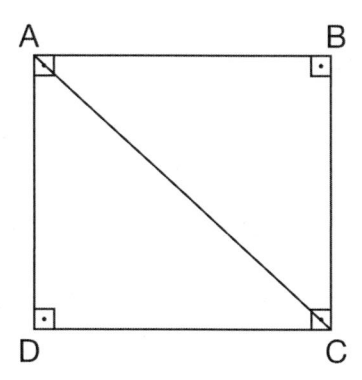

A) 4

B) 8

C) 12

D) 16

E) 15

10. The perimeter of a rectangle is P = 2L + 2W. What is the width in terms of the length and perimeter?

A) $\dfrac{P}{2} + L$

B) $\dfrac{P}{2} - L$

C) P + L

D) P − 2L

E) P + 2L

Area & Perimeter Test 16
Answer Key

1)	C
2)	B
3)	D
4)	A
5)	D
6)	C
7)	A
8)	C
9)	A
10)	B

Area & Perimeter Test 16
Solutions

1.

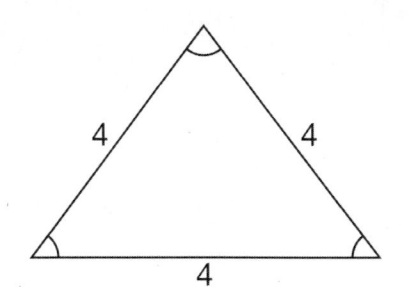

Area = $\dfrac{a^2\sqrt{3}}{4}$

Area = $\dfrac{(4)^2\sqrt{3}}{4}$

$= \dfrac{16\sqrt{3}}{4} = 4\sqrt{3}$

Correct Answer : C

2.

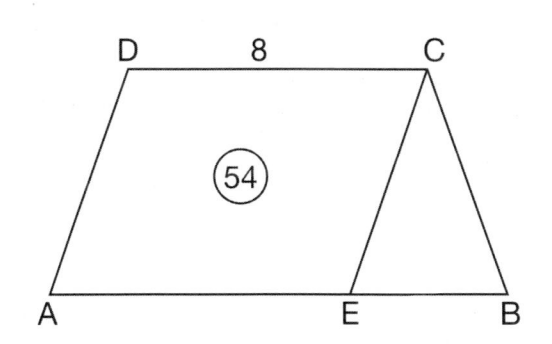

$\dfrac{x}{27} = \dfrac{4}{8}$

$x = 13 \cdot 5 \text{ cm}^2$

Correct Answer : B

3.

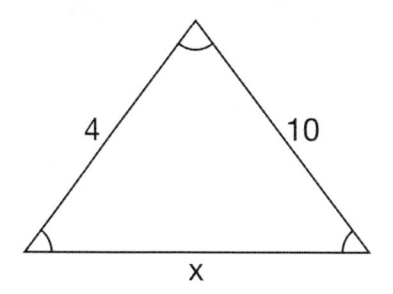

$10 - 4 < x < 10 + 4$

$6 < x < 14$

Correct Answer : D

4.

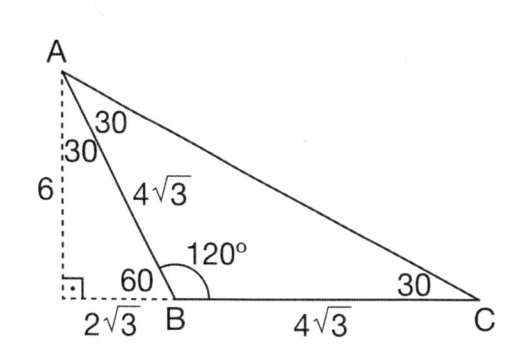

$30° \longrightarrow 2\sqrt{3}$

$60° \longrightarrow 6$

Area $= \dfrac{h \cdot b}{2} = \dfrac{6 \cdot 4\sqrt{3}}{2}$

$= 12\sqrt{3}$

Correct Answer : A

129

Area & Perimeter Test 16
Solutions

5.

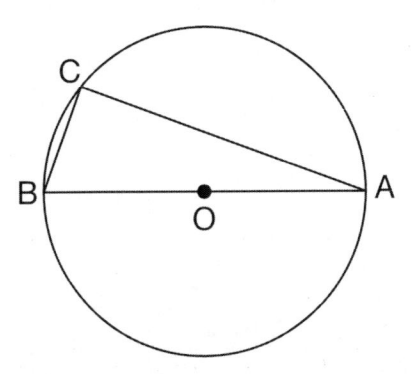

Pythogorean theorem
$(BC)^2 + (AC)^2 = (BA)^2$
$12^2 + (AC)^2 = 20^2$ AC = 16 cm
$A(ABC) = \dfrac{12 \cdot 16}{2} = 96$ cm^2

Correct Answer : D

6.

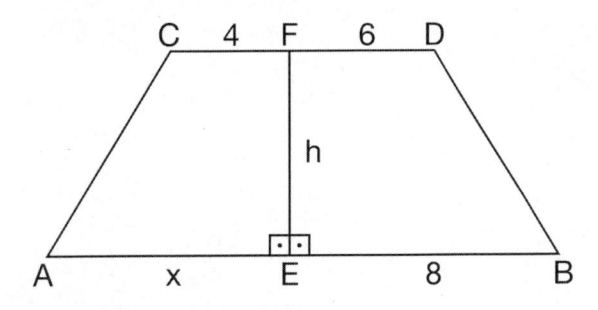

if A(AEFC) = A(EBDF)

$\dfrac{(6+8)h}{2} = \dfrac{(4+x)h}{2}$

$\dfrac{14}{2} = \dfrac{4+x}{2}$

14 = 4 + x   10 = x

Correct Answer : C

7. $4k + 5k + 9k = 180°$
$18k = 180°$
$k = 10°$
smallest angle = 4k
= 40°

Correct Answer : A

8.

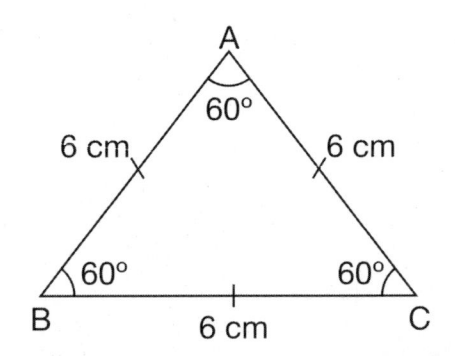

Area = $\dfrac{a^2\sqrt{3}}{4}$

= $\dfrac{36\sqrt{3}}{4} = 9\sqrt{3}$

Correct Answer : C

9.

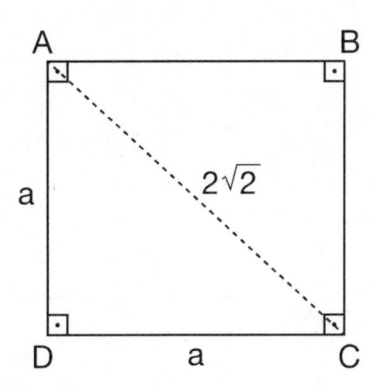

$a^2 + a^2 = (2\sqrt{2})^2$
$2a^2 = 8$
$a^2 = 4$
$a = 2$
Area of square = $a^2 = 4$

Correct Answer : A

10. P = 2L + 2W

$W = \dfrac{P - 2L}{2} = \dfrac{P}{2} - L$

Correct Answer : B

Circle Test 17

1. In the following figure, what is the measure of x?

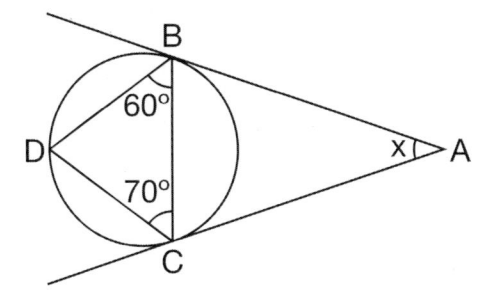

A) 60°
B) 75°
C) 80°
D) 95°
E) 105°

2. If the circumference of a circle is 12π, what is the area of the circle?

A) 6π
B) 12π
C) 24π
D) 36π
E) 42π

3. In the following figure O is the center of circle, what is the measure of ∠(ABC)?

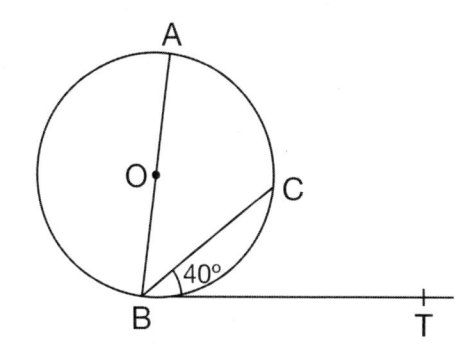

A) 40°
B) 50°
C) 60°
D) 80°
E) 85°

4. In the following figure O is the center of circle, what is the measure of x?

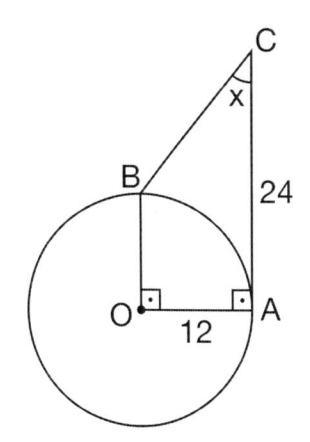

A) 15°
B) 25°
C) 30°
D) 45°
E) 50°

Circle Test 17

5. In the following figure, what is the measure of a?

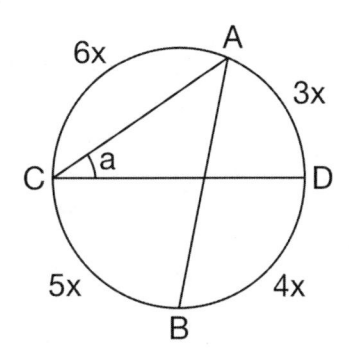

- A) 15°
- B) 25°
- C) 30°
- D) 45°
- E) 50°

6. In the following figure, what is the measure of x?

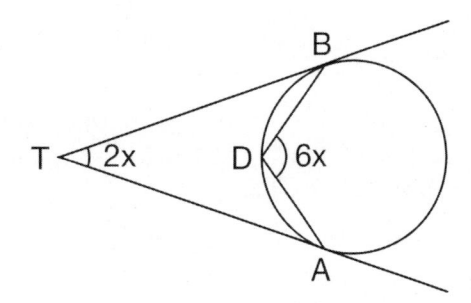

- A) 6
- B) 12
- C) 18
- D) 24
- E) 28

7. In the figure below, AB and CE are diameters of the circles. What is the measure of x?

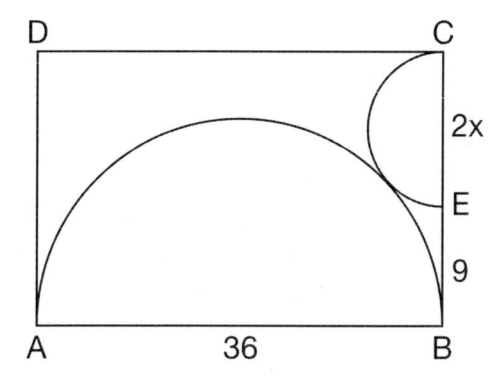

- A) 1
- B) 3
- C) 4.5
- D) 5
- E) 6

8. In the following figure P is the center of circle, find the area of the shaded region.

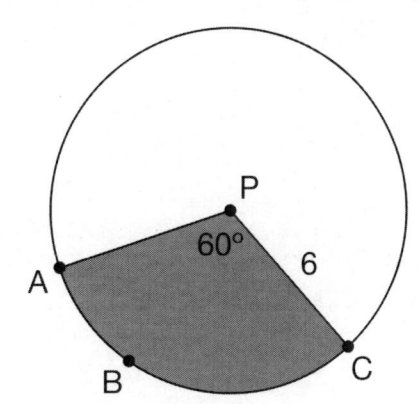

- A) 3π
- B) 6π
- C) 9π
- D) 12π
- E) 15π

Circle Test 17

9. In the following figure O is the center of circle, find the length of the arc AC

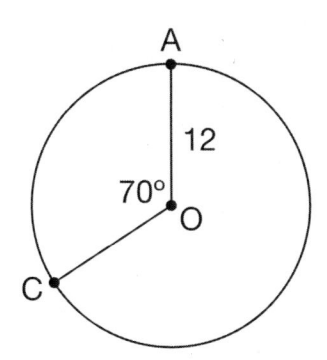

A) $\dfrac{14}{3}\pi$

B) $\dfrac{3\pi}{14}$

C) 3π

D) 14π

E) 18π

10. If the ratio of the circumference to the area of a circle is 4 to 6, what is the radius of the circle?

A) 1
B) 3
C) 4
D) 6
E) 7

11. Find the area of the shaded region.

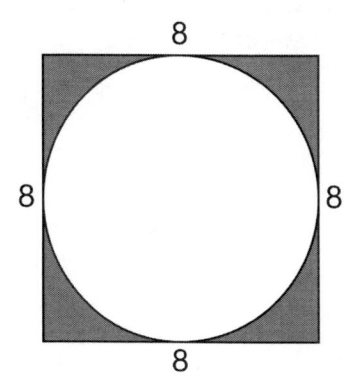

A) $64 - 32\pi$
B) $64 - 16\pi$
C) $32\pi - 64$
D) $16 - 32\pi$
E) $12 - 16\pi$

12. If the bigger circle has a center at O and a daimeter of 16 inches, find the area of the shaded part.

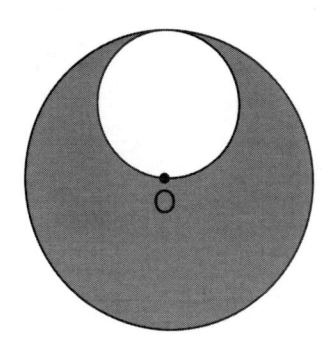

A) 12π
B) 24π
C) 32π
D) 48π
E) 52π

133

Circle Test 17

13. If the center of a circle is at (3,6), and the radius of the circle is 4, what is the equation of that circle?

A) $(x-3)^2 + (y-6)^2 = 4$

B) $(x-3)^2 + (y-6)^2 = 8$

C) $(x-3)^2 + (y-6)^2 = 16$

D) $(x-6)^2 + (y-3)^2 = 4$

E) $(x-3)^2 + (y-4)^2 = 36$

14. In the following figure O is the center of circle, find the area of the shaded part.

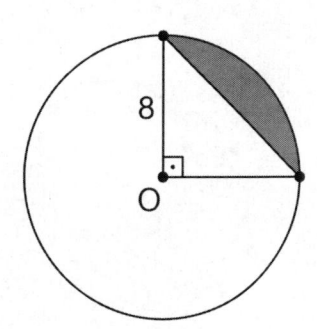

A) $16 - 32\pi$

B) $16\pi - 32$

C) 32π

D) 16π

E) 18π

Circle Test 17
Answer Key

1)	C
2)	D
3)	B
4)	D
5)	C
6)	C
7)	C
8)	B
9)	A
10)	B
11)	B
12)	D
13)	C
14)	B

Circle Test 17
Solutions

1.

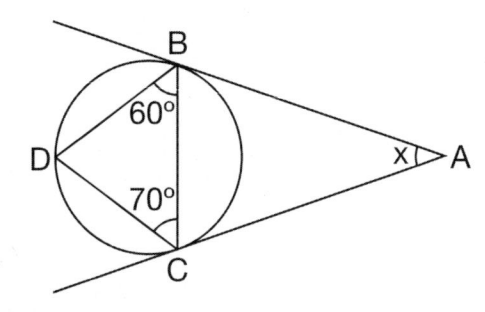

ArcBD = 140°

ArcDC = 120°

ArcBC = m°

m + 140° + 120° = 360°

m = 100°

x = 180° − m

x = 80°

Correct Answer : C

2. C = 2πr

2πr = 12π

2r = 12

r = 6

A = πr² = 36π

Correct Answer : D

3.

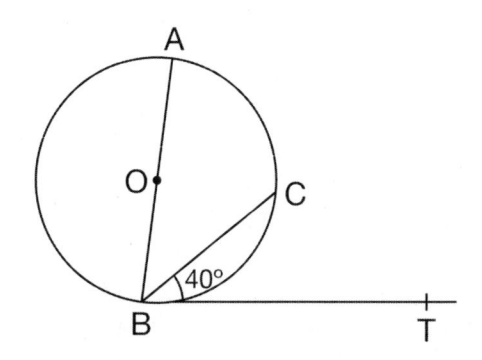

ArcBC = 80°

ArcAC = 100°

△(ABC) = $\frac{100°}{2}$ = 50°

Correct Answer : B

4.

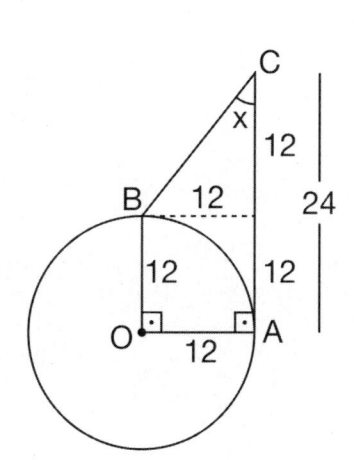

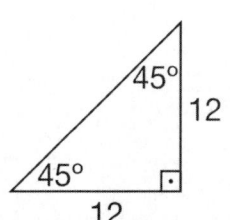

Correct Answer : D

Circle Test 17
Solutions

5.

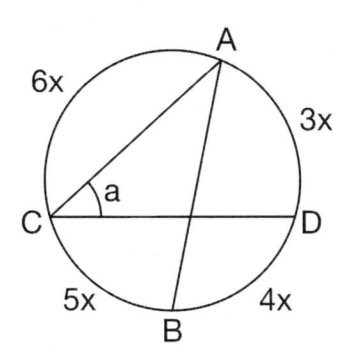

$6x + 5x + 4x + 3x = 360°$

$18x = 360°$

$x = 20°$, $2a = 3x$

$2a = 60°$, $a = 30°$

Correct Answer : C

6.

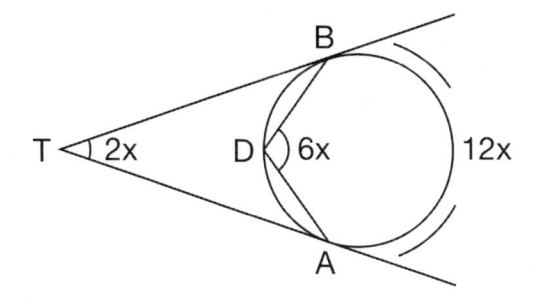

ArcADB = $360° - 12x$

$\dfrac{12x - (360 - 12x)}{2} = 2x$

$24x - 360 = 4x$

$20x = 360$

$x = 18°$

Correct Answer : C

7.

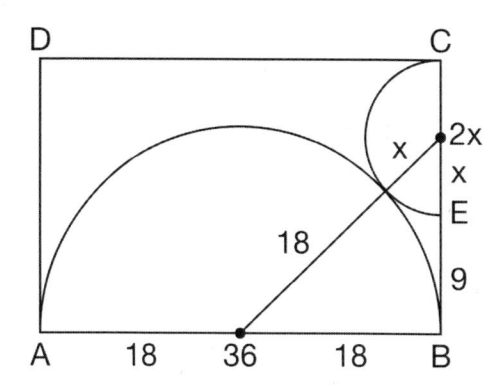

Pythagorean theorem

$(x + 9)^2 + 18^2 = (x + 18)^2$

$x^2 + 18x + 81 + 324 = x^2 + 36x + 324$

$81 = 18x$

$\dfrac{81}{18} = x$

$\dfrac{9}{2} = x$, $4.5 = x$

Correct Answer : C

8.

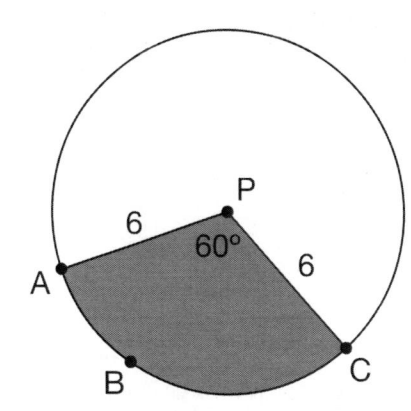

Shaded Area = $\dfrac{\pi r^2 \alpha}{360}$

$= \dfrac{\pi \cdot 36 \cdot 60}{360} = \dfrac{\pi \cdot r^2 \cdot 60°}{360°} = \dfrac{\pi \cdot 36 \cdot 60°}{360°}$

$= 6\pi$

Correct Answer : B

Circle Test 17
Solutions

9.

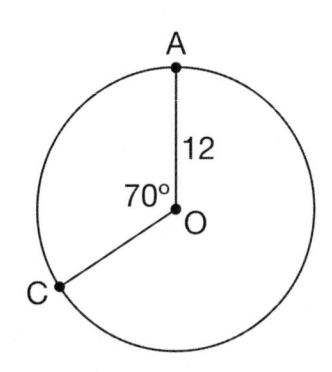

$$\text{ArcAC} = \frac{2\pi r \alpha}{360}$$

$$= \frac{2\pi r 70°}{360°} = \frac{2\pi \cdot 12 \cdot 70°}{360°}$$

$$= \frac{14}{3}\pi$$

Correct Answer : A

10. $\dfrac{\text{ratio of circumference}}{\text{ratio of area}}$

$$\frac{2\pi r}{\pi r^2} = \frac{4}{6}$$

$$\frac{2r}{r^2} = \frac{4}{6}$$

$$\frac{2}{r} = \frac{4}{6}, \ r = 3$$

Correct Answer : B

11.

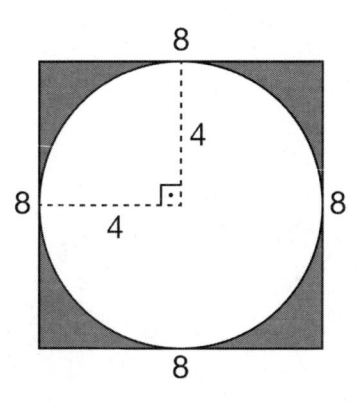

$A(ABCD) = 8 \cdot 8 = 64$

Area of Circle $= \pi r^2 = 16\pi$

Shaded Area $= 64 - 16\pi$

Correct Answer : B

12.

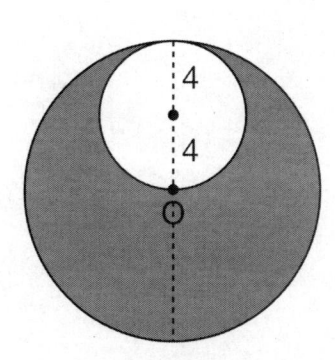

Small Circle Area $= \pi r^2 = 16\pi$

Big Circle Area $= \pi r^2 = 64\pi$

Shaded Area $= 64\pi - 16\pi$

$= 48\pi$

Correct Answer : D

138

Circle Test 17
Solutions

13. $(x - h)^2 + (y - k)^2 = r^2$

$(x - 3)^2 + (y - 6)^2 = 16$

Correct Answer : C

14.

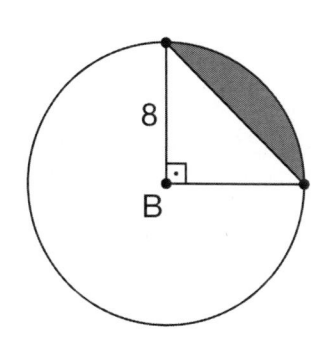

$A(ABC) = \dfrac{8 \cdot 8}{2} = 32$

Area of Quarter of Circle

$= \dfrac{\pi r^2}{4} = \dfrac{64\pi}{4} = 16\pi$

Shaded Area $= 16\pi - 32$

Correct Answer : B

Volume Test 18

1.

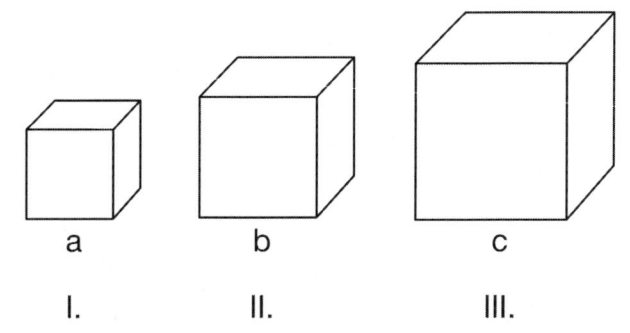

There are three cubes given above. Their side length is given under the cubes. 'I' is a, 'II' is b, 'III' is c. Their volumes are V_a, V_b, and V_c.

$$c = 2b = 3a$$

$\frac{1}{V_a} + \frac{1}{V_b} + \frac{1}{V_c} = \frac{1}{6}$, then find volume of V_c = ?

A) 216
B) 125
C) 64
D) 27
E) 25

2. The radius of the sphare below is 6 cm. What is the voluma of the sphere?

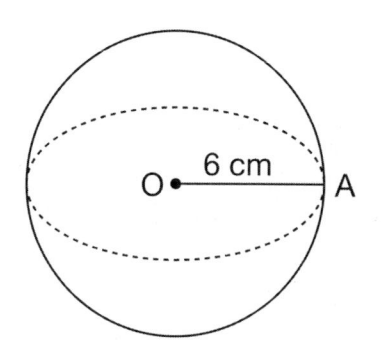

A) $128\pi \, cm^2$
B) $142\pi \, cm^2$
C) $208\pi \, cm^2$
D) $225\pi \, cm^2$
E) $288\pi \, cm^2$

3. In the following cylinder shape, if the volume of the cylinder $72\pi \, cm^3$, find the radius of the cylinder.

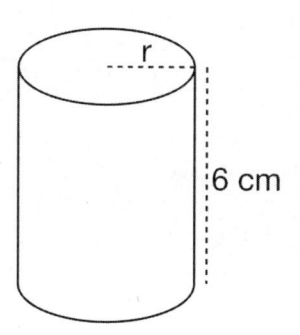

A) $\sqrt{3}$ cm
B) $2\sqrt{3}$ cm
C) $3\sqrt{3}$ cm
D) 6 cm
E) 8 cm

Volume Test 18

4. In the following figures, the volume of the cone and the cylinder are equal. What is the value of a?

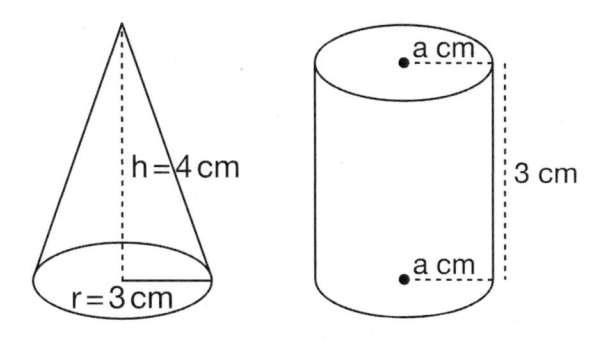

- A) 1 cm
- B) 2 cm
- C) 3 cm
- D) 4 cm
- E) 6 cm

5. A cube has a volume of 27 ft³. What is the one side of cube?

- A) 1 ft
- B) 2 ft
- C) 3 ft
- D) 4 ft
- E) 8 ft

6. The radius of a cylinder is increased by 25% and its height is decreased by 20%. What is the effect on the volume of the cylinder?

- A) It is decreased by 50%
- B) It is decreased by 25%
- C) It is increased by 25%
- D) It is increased by 50%
- E) It is increased by 45%

7. A cylinder has a height that is four times as long as its radius. If the volume of the cylinder is 32π cm³ then find the radius.

- A) 1 cm
- B) 2 cm
- C) 3 cm
- D) 4 cm
- E) 6 cm

141

Volume Test 18

8. The following cone has a diameter of 16ft and a height of 18ft. Find the volume of the cone? (Give your answer in terms of π)

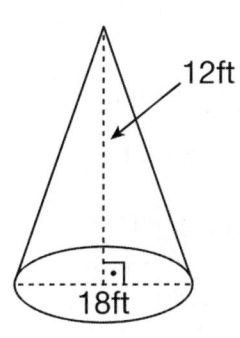

A) 150π ft³

B) 196π ft³

C) 324π ft³

D) 480π ft³

E) 560π ft³

9. A cylinder has a height of 4 cm and a volume of 64π cm³. What is the radius of the cylinder?

A) 4 cm

B) 8 cm

C) 10 cm

D) 24 cm

E) 28 cm

10. Find the volume of the following pyramid.

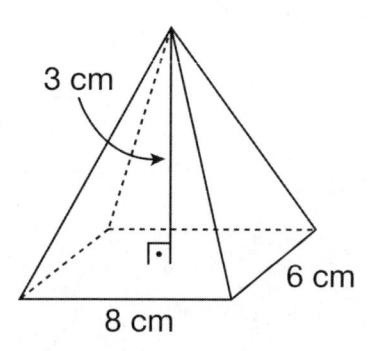

A) 12 cm³

B) 24 cm³

C) 48 cm³

D) 60 cm³

E) 72 cm³

142

Volume Test 18
Answer Key

1)	A
2)	E
3)	B
4)	B
5)	C
6)	C
7)	B
8)	C
9)	A
10)	C

Volume Test 18
Solutions

1. Let $a = 2k, b = 3k, c = 6k$

$\dfrac{1}{8k^3} + \dfrac{1}{27k^3} + \dfrac{1}{216k^3} = \dfrac{1}{6}$

$\dfrac{36}{216k^3} = \dfrac{1}{6}$, $216k^3 = 216$

$k^3 = 1$

$k = 1$

$V_c = 216k^3 = 216$

Correct Answer : A

2. $V = \dfrac{4}{3}\pi r^3$

$V = \dfrac{4}{3}\pi(6)^3 = \dfrac{4}{3}\pi(6\,cm \cdot 6\,cm \cdot 6\,cm) = 288\pi\,cm^3$

Correct Answer : E

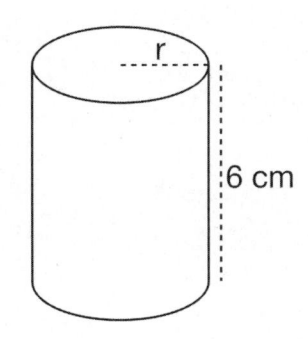

3.

Volume of cylinder $= \pi r^2 h$

$\pi r^2 \cdot 6\,cm = 72\pi\,cm^3$

$r^2 \cdot 6\,cm = 72\,cm^3$

$r^2 = \dfrac{72\,cm^3}{6\,cm}$, $r^2 = 12\,cm^2$

$r = 2\sqrt{3}\,cm$

Correct Answer : B

4.

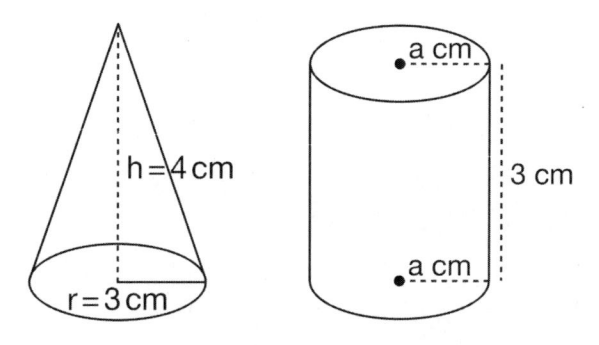

$V_{cone} = \dfrac{1}{3}\pi r^2 h = \dfrac{1}{3}\pi \cdot 9 \cdot 4 = 12\pi$

$V_{cylinder} = \pi r^2 h = \pi \cdot a^2 \cdot 3$

$= \pi \cdot a^2 \cdot 3$

$V_{cone} = V_{cylinder}$

$12\pi = \pi \cdot a^2 \cdot 3$

$\dfrac{12}{3} = a^2$, $a^2 = 4$, $a = 2\,cm$

Correct Answer : B

5. $V = a^3$

$27\,ft^3 = a^3$

$3\,ft = a$

Correct Answer : C

6. Suppose $r = 4$ $V = \pi r^2$

$h = 5$ $V = \pi \cdot 16 \cdot 5 = 80\pi$

$r \longrightarrow 25\%$ increase $r = 5$

$h \longrightarrow 20\%$ decrease $h = 4$

$V = \pi r^2 = 25 \times 4 \times \pi = 100\pi$

$\dfrac{100\pi - 80\pi}{80\pi} = \dfrac{1}{4} = 25\%$ increase

Correct Answer : C

Volume Test 18
Solutions

7. $r = x$

$h = 4x$

$V = \pi r^2 h$

$V = \pi \cdot x^2 \cdot 4x$

$\quad = 4x^3 \pi$

Since $V = 32\pi$

$\quad 4x^3 \pi = 32\pi$

$\quad 4x^3 \pi = 32\pi$

$\quad\quad 4x^3 = 32$

$\quad\quad\quad x^3 = 8$

$\quad\quad\quad\; x = 2$

Correct Answer : B

8.

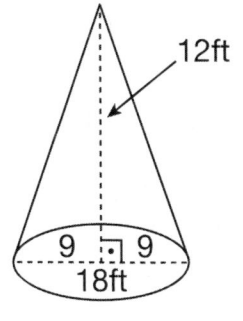

$V = \dfrac{1}{3}\pi r^2 h$

$V = \dfrac{1}{3}\pi \cdot 81 \cdot 12$

$V = 324\pi \, ft^3$

Correct Answer : C

9. $h = 4$ cm

$V = 64$ cm^3

$V = \pi r^2 h$

$64\pi = \pi \cdot r^2 \cdot 4$, $r^2 = 16$ cm^2

$r = 4$ cm

Correct Answer : A

10.

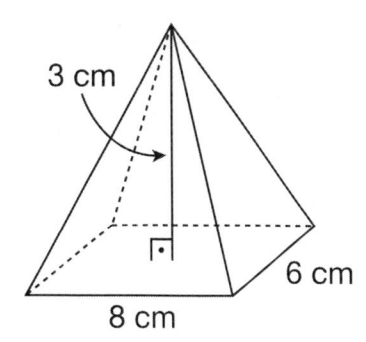

$V_{pyramid} = \dfrac{l \cdot w \cdot h}{3}$

$V = \dfrac{3\,cm \cdot 6\,cm \cdot 8\,cm}{3}$

$V = 48 \, cm^3$

Correct Answer : C

Mixed Review Test IV

1.

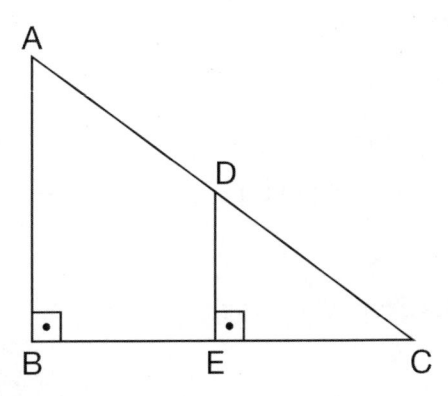

AB // DE
|AB| = 8
|BC| = 6
|DE| = 4, then find |DC| + |EC| ?

A) 5
B) 6
C) 7
D) 8
E) 10

2.

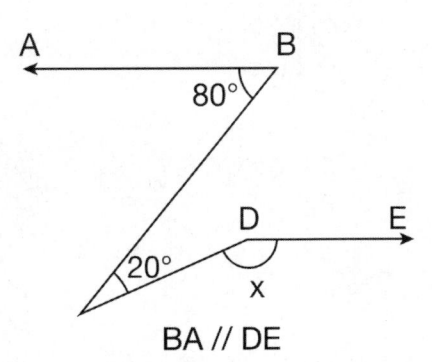

BA // DE
What is the value of x?

A) 70°
B) 90°
C) 110°
D) 120°
E) 130°

3.

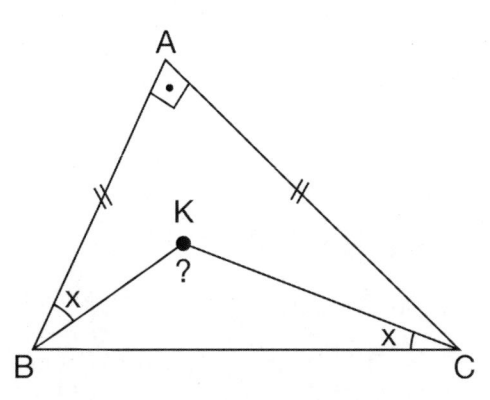

Find the angle of ∠(BKC).

A) 120°
B) 150°
C) 130°
D) 132°
E) 135°

4.

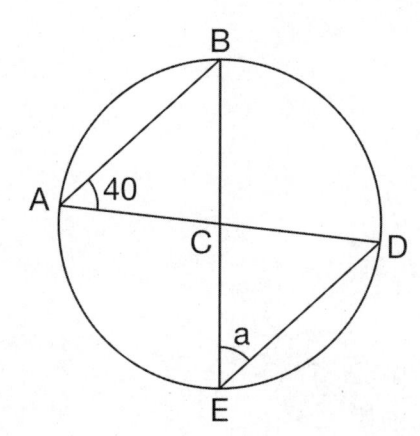

If C is the center of the circle then find the a° = ?

A) 30°
B) 40°
C) 50°
D) 60°
E) 70°

146

Mixed Review Test IV

5.

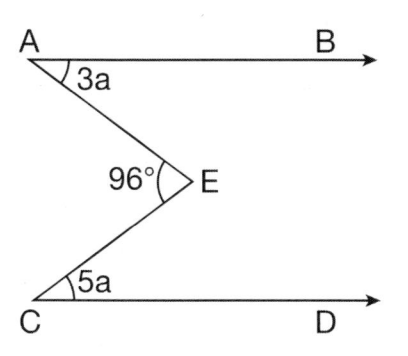

In the figure above, AB is parallel to CD. What is the angle of ∠(BAE)?

A) 10°
B) 20°
C) 25°
D) 32°
E) 36°

6.

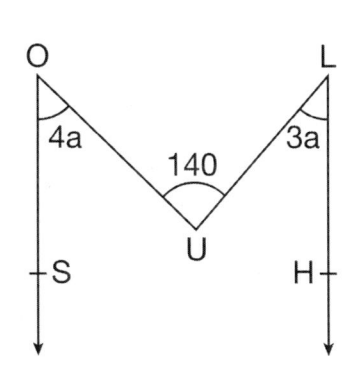

OS // LH

$m(\widehat{SOU}) = 4a$ ∠(ULH) = 3a ∠(OUL) = 140

So what is the value of 2a?

A) 30
B) 40
C) 50
D) 80
E) 85

7.

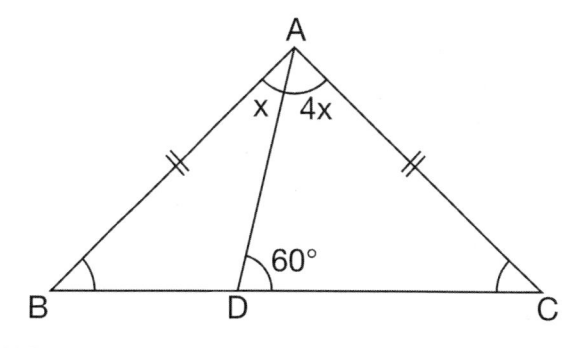

What is the value of x?

A) 10°
B) 20°
C) 30°
D) 40°
E) 50°

8.

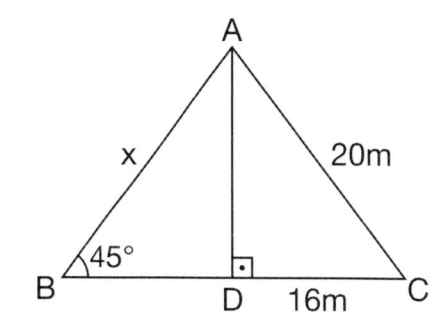

|AC| = 20m
|DC| = 16m
$m(\widehat{ABD}) = 45°$

What is tle length of x?

A) 8m
B) $8\sqrt{2}$ m
C) $12\sqrt{2}$ m
D) 16m
E) 18m

147

Mixed Review Test IV

9.

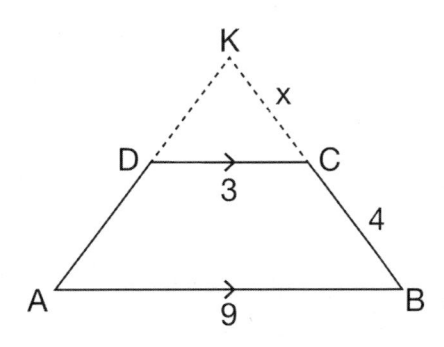

If DC // AB in the above figure, what is the value of x?

A) 2
B) 4
C) 6
D) 8
E) 10

10. Find the value of x in the diagram

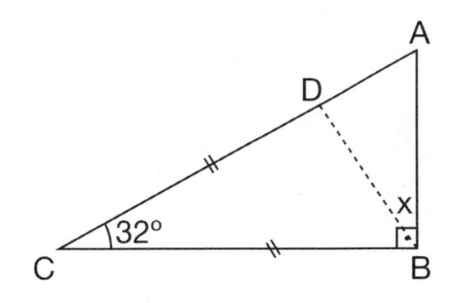

A) 13°
B) 16°
C) 36°
D) 38°
E) 42°

11.

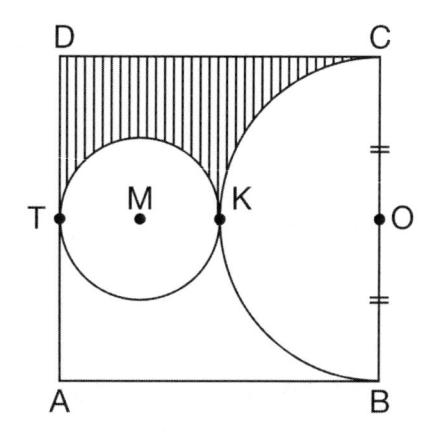

In the following figures, M and O are center of circles, ABCD is a square and AB = 4 feet.

What is the area of the shaded part?

A) $8 - \dfrac{3\pi}{2}$
B) $4 - \dfrac{3\pi}{2}$
C) $\dfrac{3\pi}{2} - 2$
D) $\dfrac{3\pi}{2}$
E) $\dfrac{3}{4}\pi$

12. Find the volume of a rectangular prism that has a length of 6 cm, a width of 4 cm, and a height of 10 cm.

A) 60 cm³
B) 120 cm³
C) 240 cm³
D) 480 cm³
E) 560 cm³

Mixed Review Test IV
Answer Key

1)	D
2)	D
3)	E
4)	B
5)	E
6)	B
7)	B
8)	C
9)	A
10)	B
11)	A
12)	C

Mixed Review Test IV
Solutions

1.

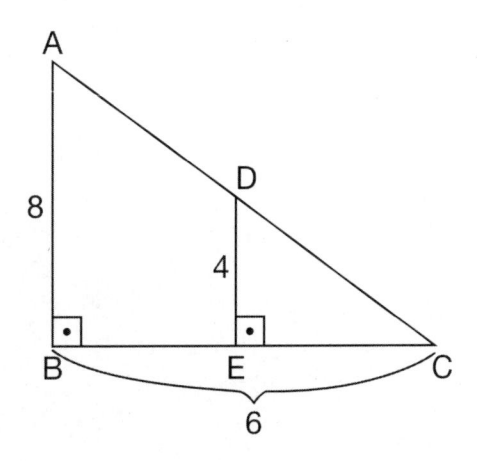

$|AC| = 6^2 + 8^2 = 10^2$

$|AC| = 10$

$\dfrac{4}{8} = \dfrac{|DC|}{|AC|}$, $\dfrac{1}{2} = \dfrac{|DC|}{10}$

$|DC| = 5$

$\dfrac{1}{2} = \dfrac{|EC|}{|BC|}$, $\dfrac{1}{2} = \dfrac{|EC|}{6}$

$|EC| = 3$

$|DC| + |EC| = 5 + 3 = 8$

Correct Answer : D

2.

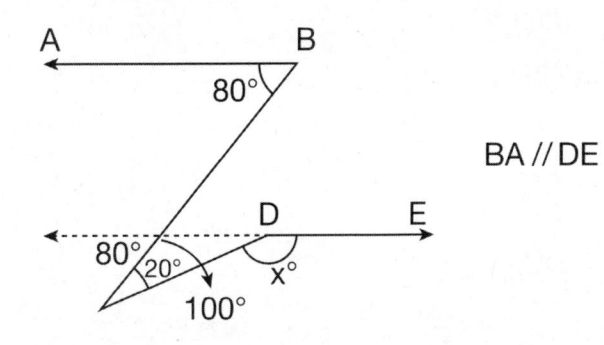

BA // DE

$x° = 100° + 20°$

$x = 120°$

Correct Answer : D

3.

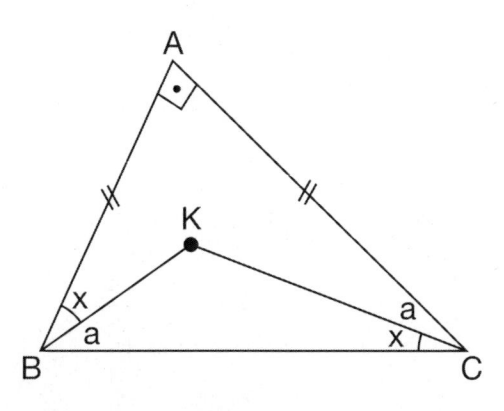

$2x + 2a + 90° = 180°$

$x + a = 45°$

$<(BCK) + x + a = 180°$

$<(BCK) + 45° = 180°$

$<(BCK) = 135°$

Correct Answer : E

4. If $\angle (A) = 40°$ then

ArcBD = 80°

$a° = \dfrac{ArcBD}{2} = \dfrac{80°}{2}$

$a° = 40°$

Correct Answer : B

5. $3\alpha + 5\alpha = 96°$

$8\alpha = 96° \longrightarrow \alpha = 12° \longrightarrow \angle (BAE) = 3a$
$= 3 \cdot 12$
$= 36°$

Correct Answer : E

6. Since OS // LH $4a + 3a = 140$

$7a = 140$

$a = 20$, then $2a = 40$

Correct Answer : B

150

Mixed Review Test IV
Solutions

7.

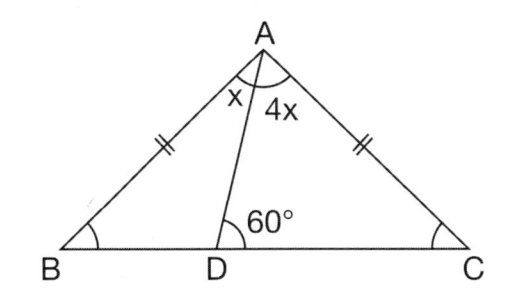

$x + n = 60°$

$5x + 2n = 180°$ $x = 20°$

Correct Answer : B

8.

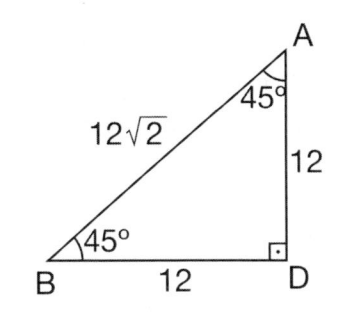

$|AD|^2 + 16^2 = 20^2$

$|AD| = 12m$

$s(\widehat{BAC}) = 45°$, then $|BD| = 12m$

$|AB| = x = 12\sqrt{2}\,m$

Correct Answer : C

9. From similarity theorem

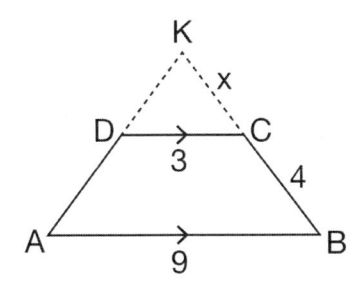

$\dfrac{x}{x+4} = \dfrac{3}{9}$

$\dfrac{x}{x+4} = \dfrac{1}{3}$ (cross multiply)

$3x = x + 4$

$3x - x = 4$

$2x = 4$

$x = 2$

Correct Answer : A

10.

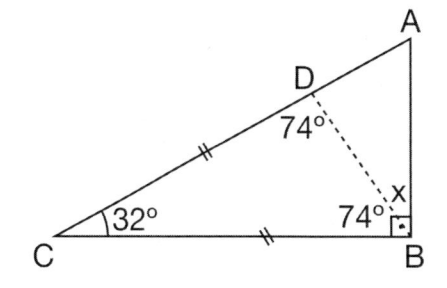

$\dfrac{180 - 32}{2} = \dfrac{148}{2} = 74°$

$x + 74 = 90$ $x = 16$

Correct Answer : B

11. $A(ABCD) = 4^2 = 16\,ft^2$

$A(TDCO) = 4 \cdot 2 = 8\,ft^2$

Area of small half circle = $\dfrac{\pi r^2}{2} = \dfrac{\pi}{2}$

Area of quarter of big circle = $\dfrac{\pi r^2}{2} = \dfrac{\pi \cdot 2^2}{4} = \pi$

Shaded area = $8 - \left(\dfrac{\pi}{2} + \pi\right) = 8 - \dfrac{3\pi}{2}$

Correct Answer : A

12. $V_{rectangular\ prism} = l \cdot w \cdot h$

$V = 4\,cm \cdot 6\,cm \cdot 10\,cm$

$V = 240\,cm^3$

Correct Answer : C

CHAPTER V PRE-CALCULUS
Trigonometry Test 19

1. Solve $(\tan\alpha \cdot \cos\alpha)^2 + (\sin\alpha \cdot \cot\alpha)^2$.

A) $\sin\alpha$

B) $\cos\alpha$

C) 1

D) $\tan\alpha$

E) $\cot\alpha$

2. Find $\cos 30° \cdot \sin 60° \cdot \tan 60°$?

A) $\dfrac{\sqrt{3}}{3}$

B) $\dfrac{3}{4}$

C) $\sqrt{3}$

D) $\dfrac{3\sqrt{3}}{4}$

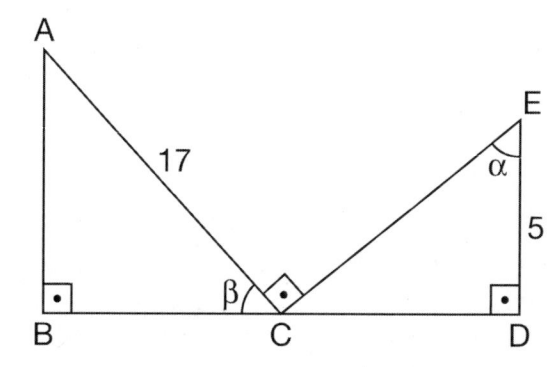

E) $\dfrac{\sqrt{3}}{4}$

3.

If $AB \perp BC$

$ED \perp CD$

$AC \perp CE$

$|BD| = 27$

$|AB| = 8$

$|AC| = 17$

$|ED| = 5$

From the above triangles, find $\sin\alpha \cdot \cot\beta$?

A) $\dfrac{29}{45}$

B) $\dfrac{45}{29}$

C) $\dfrac{26}{45}$

D) $\dfrac{45}{26}$

E) $\dfrac{31}{45}$

Trigonometry Test 19

4. In a right triangle, one angle measures x°, where $\cos x° = \frac{5}{13}$.
What is the $\tan(90 - x°)$?

A) $\frac{12}{13}$

B) $\frac{5}{12}$

C) $\frac{7}{12}$

D) $\frac{13}{12}$

E) $\frac{17}{19}$

5. $\frac{7\sin x° + 2\cos x°}{4\cos x° + 5\sin x°} = \frac{3}{5}$, then what is $\cot x°$?

A) 7

B) 9

C) 10

D) 11

E) 13

6. In a right triangle, the cosine of angle B is $\frac{3}{5}$ and the sine of angle B is $\frac{4}{5}$.
What is the ratio of the longest side to the shortest side?

A) $\frac{4}{3}$

B) $\frac{4}{5}$

C) $\frac{3}{4}$

D) $\frac{5}{3}$

E) $\frac{5}{4}$

7. $\tan x + \frac{\cos x}{1 + \sin x}$ what is the simplest form of the given equation?

A) $\sec x$

B) $\csc x$

C) $\cot x$

D) $\sin 2x$

E) $\cos \alpha$

8. For the following right triangle, what is the sine of angle A?

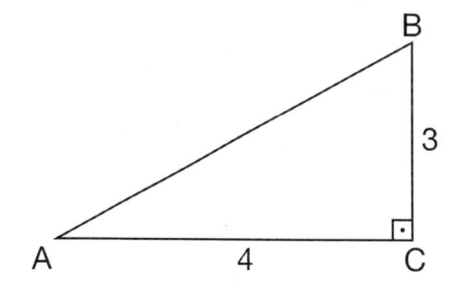

A) 3

B) 4

C) $\frac{3}{5}$

D) 5

E) 7

153

Trigonometry Test 19

9. Find $\dfrac{\cos 67° \cdot \cot 16°}{\tan 74° \cdot \sin 23°}$?

A) $\dfrac{3}{5}$

B) 1

C) 2

D) 3

E) 5

10. In the right triangle below, which of the following is correct?

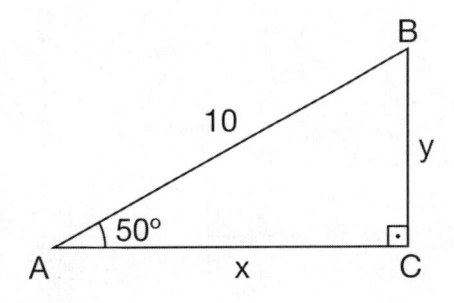

A) $\sin 50° = \dfrac{x}{y}$

B) $\tan 50° = \dfrac{y}{x}$

C) $\sin 50° = \dfrac{10}{x}$

D) $\cos 50° = \dfrac{10}{y}$

E) $\sin 40° = \dfrac{y}{10}$

11. Simplify $\sin\theta \cdot \cot\theta$

A) $\tan\theta$

B) $\cot\theta$

C) $\sin\theta$

D) $\cos\theta$

E) $\operatorname{Cosecant}\theta$

12. Convert 60° into radians measure? (Give your answer in terms of π)

A) $\dfrac{1}{3}\pi$

B) 3π

C) 2π

D) $\dfrac{1}{2}\pi$

E) 4π

154

Trigonometry Test 19
Answer Key

1)	C
2)	D
3)	D
4)	B
5)	C
6)	D
7)	A
8)	C
9)	B
10)	B
11)	D
12)	A

Trigonometry Test 19
Solutions

1. $\left(\dfrac{\sin\alpha}{\cos\alpha}\cdot\cos\alpha\right)^2+\left(\sin\alpha\cdot\dfrac{\cos\alpha}{\sin\alpha}\right)^2=$

$\sin\alpha^2+\cos\alpha^2=1$

Correct Answer : C

2. $\cos30°\cdot\sin60°\cdot\tan60°$

$=\dfrac{\sqrt{3}}{2}\cdot\dfrac{\sqrt{3}}{2}\cdot\sqrt{3}$

$=\dfrac{3\sqrt{3}}{4}$

Correct Answer : D

3. We know $|BD|=27, |BC|=15$

$|CD|=27-15=12$ then $|CE|=13$

$\sin\alpha=\dfrac{12}{13}$

$\cot\beta=\dfrac{15}{8}$

$\sin\alpha\cdot\cot\beta=\dfrac{12}{13}\cdot\dfrac{15}{8}=\dfrac{45}{26}$

Correct Answer : D

4.

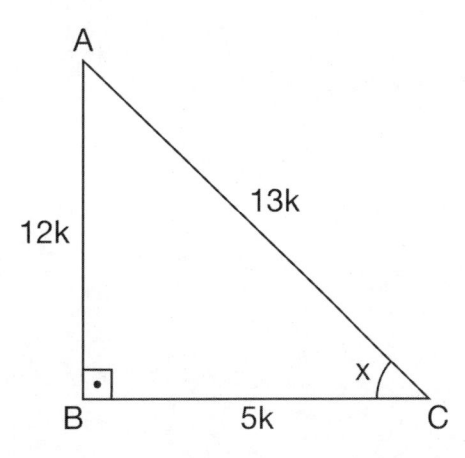

[Right triangle with vertices A (top), B (bottom-left, right angle), C (bottom-right with angle x); AB = 12k, BC = 5k, AC = 13k]

$\tan(90-x°)=\cot x°=\dfrac{5k}{12k}=\dfrac{5}{12}$

Correct Answer : B

5. $35\sin x° + 10\cos x° = 12\cos x° + 15\sin x°$

$20\sin x° = 2\cos x°$

$10\sin x° = \cos x°$

$10 = \dfrac{\cos x°}{\sin x°}$

$\cot x° = \dfrac{\cos x°}{\sin x°} = 10$

Correct Answer : C

6. $\text{Cosine } B = \dfrac{\text{adjacent}}{\text{hypotenuse}} = \dfrac{3}{5}$

$\text{Sine } B = \dfrac{\text{opposite}}{\text{hypotenuse}} = \dfrac{4}{5}$

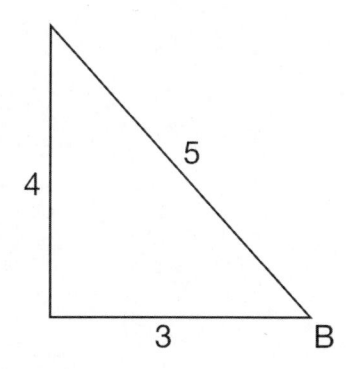

[Right triangle with legs 4 (vertical) and 3 (horizontal), hypotenuse 5, angle B at bottom-right]

Ratio of the largest side to the shortest side

$=\dfrac{5}{3}$, or 5 to 3.

Correct Answer : D

156

Trigonometry Test 19
Solutions

7. $\dfrac{\sin x}{\cos x} + \dfrac{\cos x}{1+\sin x} = \dfrac{\sin x + \sin^2 x + \cos^2 x}{\cos x (1+\sin x)}$

$= \dfrac{\cancel{1+\sin x}}{\cos x \cancel{(1+\sin x)}} = \dfrac{1}{\cos x} = \sec x$

Correct Answer : A

8.

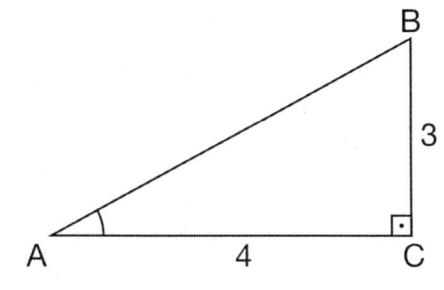

$\sin A = \dfrac{\text{Opposite}}{\text{Hypotenuse}}$

$\sin A = \dfrac{3}{5}$

Correct Answer : C

9. $\cos 67° = \sin 23°$

$\cot 16° = \tan 74°$

$\dfrac{\cancel{\sin 23°} \cdot \cancel{\tan 74°}}{\cancel{\tan 74°} \cdot \cancel{\sin 23°}} = 1$

Correct Answer : B

10.

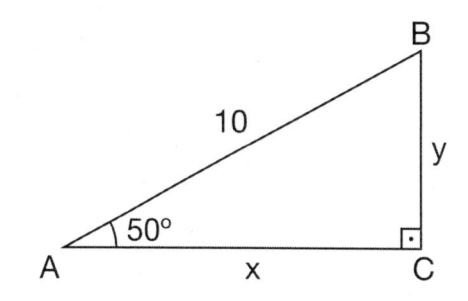

$\tan 50° = \dfrac{\sin 50°}{\cos 50°} = \dfrac{y}{x}$

Correct Answer : B

11. $\sin\theta \cdot \cot\theta$

$\sin\theta \cdot \dfrac{\cos\theta}{\sin\theta}$

$\cancel{\sin\theta} \cdot \dfrac{\cos\theta}{\cancel{\sin\theta}}$

$= \cos\theta$

Correct Answer : D

12. $\dfrac{60°}{180°} = \dfrac{R}{\pi}$, $R = \dfrac{1}{3}\pi$

Correct Answer : A

Logarithms Test 20

1. What is the value of x if $\log_2(3x-1) = 5$?

A) 5
B) 7
C) 9
D) 11
E) 13

2. What is the value of x in the equation $\log_2(x-2) + \log_2(x+3) = \log_2 6$

A) 1
B) 2
C) 3
D) 4
E) 5

3. Simplify $\log_3 40 - \log_3 5$.

A) $\log_3 2$
B) $3\log_3 2$
C) $2\log_3 2$
D) $3\log_3 4$
E) $2\log_2 3$

4. Evaluate the logarithm $\dfrac{3\log_5 27}{4\log_5 3}$.

A) 4
B) 9
C) 11
D) $\dfrac{4}{9}$
E) $\dfrac{9}{4}$

5. If $\log_n m = x$ and $\log_b m = y$, which of following could be correct?

A) $x = y$
B) $n^x = b^y$
C) $m = \dfrac{x}{y}$
D) $x^n = y^b$
E) $m = \dfrac{nx}{by}$

6. If x and y are positive integers and $\log_x 25 = 2$ and $\log_5 x = y$, then find $x \cdot y = ?$

A) 1
B) 3
C) 4
D) 5
E) 7

158

Logarithms Test 20

7. If $\log_{10}40 - \log_{10}(x+1) = 1$, then find x?

A) 0
B) 1
C) 2
D) 3
E) 4

8. Evaluate $\log x^y \cdot \log_y z \cdot \log_z k$

A) $\dfrac{\log k}{\log x}$
B) $\dfrac{\log x}{\log y}$
C) $\log y$
D) $\log z$
E) $\log k$

9. If $\cdot \log_{25} y = \dfrac{3}{2}$, then y = ?

A) 5
B) 25
C) 125
D) 225
E) 675

10. If $\ln x^3 = 2 + \ln y^5$, then express x in terms of y.

A) $x = \sqrt[3]{e^2 \cdot y^5}$
B) $x = \sqrt[3]{e^3 \cdot y^3}$
C) $x = \sqrt[3]{e^5 \cdot y^5}$
D) $x = \sqrt[3]{e^4 \cdot y^5}$
E) $x = \sqrt[3]{e^4 \cdot y^5}$

11. If $\log_8(3x-1) - \log_8(2x+1) = 0$, then find x = ?

A) 1
B) 2
C) 5
D) 8
E) 10

12. If $x > 0$ and $f(x) = 2^{x+1}$, then which of following could be $f^{-1}(x)$.

A) $\log_2$
B) $\log \dfrac{x}{2}$
C) $\log_2 \dfrac{x}{2}$
D) $\log_2 \dfrac{x}{2}$
E) $\dfrac{x}{2}$

13. Solve $\dfrac{1}{\log_4 8} + \dfrac{1}{\log_4 8} = ?$

A) $\log_8 3$
B) $\log_4 3$
C) 1
D) $\dfrac{1}{2}$
E) 3

159

Trigonometry Test 20
Answer Key

1)	D
2)	C
3)	B
4)	E
5)	B
6)	D
7)	D
8)	A
9)	C
10)	E
11)	B
12)	C
13)	C

Logarithms Test 20
Solutions

1. $\log_2(3x-1) = 5$
$3x - 1 = 2^5$
$3x - 1 = 32$
$3x = 33$
$x = 11$

Correct Answer : D

2. $\log_2(x-2) + \log_2(x+3) = \log_2 6$
$\log_2(x-2)(x+3) = \log_2 6$
$(x-2)(x+3)$
$x^2 + x - 6 = 6$
$x^2 + x - 12 = 0$
$(x-3)(x+4) = 0$, then $x = 3$ or $x = -4$, since -4 can not be solution the x can be only 3.

Correct Answer : C

3. $\log 3^{40} - \log 3^5$
$\log_3 \frac{40}{5} = \log_3 8 = \log_3 2^3 = 3\log_3 2$

Correct Answer : B

4. $\dfrac{3\log_5 27}{4\log_5 3} = \dfrac{3\log_5 3^3}{4\log_5 3} = \dfrac{9\log_5 3}{4\log_5 3} = \dfrac{9}{4}$

Correct Answer : E

5. $\log_n m = x \Rightarrow m = n^x$
$\log_b m = y \Rightarrow m = b^y$ then $n^x = b^y$

Correct Answer : B

6. $\log_x 25 = 2 \Rightarrow x^2 = 25$, then $x = 5$
$\log_5 x = y \Rightarrow 5^y = x \Rightarrow 5^y = 5^1$, then $y = 1$
$x \cdot y = 5 \cdot 1 = 5$

Correct Answer : D

Logarithms Test 20
Solutions

7. $\log 40 - \log(x+1) = 1$

$\log_{10} \dfrac{40}{x+1} = 1 \Rightarrow \dfrac{40}{x+1} = 10^1$ (cross multiply)

$40 = 10x + 10$

$30 = 10x$

$3 = x$

Correct Answer : D

8. $\dfrac{\log y}{\log x} \cdot \dfrac{\log z}{\log y} \cdot \dfrac{\log k}{\log z} = \dfrac{\log k}{\log x}$

Correct Answer : D

9. $\log_{25} y = \dfrac{3}{2}$

$y = 25^{\frac{3}{2}} \Rightarrow y = 5^3 = 125$

Correct Answer : C

10. $\ln x^3 = 2 + \ln y^5$

$\ln x^3 - \ln y^5 = 2$

$\ln \dfrac{x^3}{y^5} = 2$

$\dfrac{x^3}{y^5} = e^2 \Rightarrow x^3 = e^2 \cdot y^5$, then $x = \sqrt[3]{e^4 \cdot y^5}$

Correct Answer : E

11. $\log_8(3x-1) - \log_8(2x+1) = 0$

$\log_8 \dfrac{3x-1}{2x+1} = 0$, then $\dfrac{3x-1}{2x+1} = 8^0$

$\dfrac{3x-1}{2x+1} = 1 \Rightarrow 3x - 1 = 2x + 1$

$3x - 2x = 1 + 1$

$x = 2$

Correct Answer : B

12. Note:

$y = a^x \Leftrightarrow x = \log_a y$

$f(x) = y = 2^{2x+1} \Rightarrow y = 2^x \cdot 2^1$

$2^x = \dfrac{y}{2}$, $x = \log_2 \dfrac{y}{2}$

$f^{-1}(x) = \log_2 \dfrac{x}{2}$

Correct Answer : C

13. $\dfrac{1}{\log_4 8} + \dfrac{1}{\log_4 8} \Rightarrow \log_8 4 + \log_8 4$

$= \log_8 8 = 1$

Correct Answer : C

Matrix Test 21

1. Let K = [2 4] and L = $\begin{bmatrix} -3 & 4 \\ 2 & -1 \end{bmatrix}$, then find K · L

   A) [2, 4]
   B) [4, 2]
   C) [−2, 4]
   D) [2, −4]
   E) [−2, −4]

2. If $3\begin{bmatrix} x \\ y \end{bmatrix} = 4\begin{bmatrix} 12 \\ 18 \end{bmatrix}$, then what is value of x + y?

   A) 20
   B) 25
   C) 30
   D) 35
   E) 40

3. The matrix Y = $\begin{bmatrix} 3 & 6 \\ 4 & 7 \end{bmatrix}$ and X − Y = $\begin{bmatrix} 1 & 3 \\ 2 & 4 \end{bmatrix}$, then which of following gives matrix X?

   A) $\begin{bmatrix} 4 & 9 \\ 6 & 11 \end{bmatrix}$
   B) $\begin{bmatrix} 3 & 6 \\ 4 & 7 \end{bmatrix}$
   C) $\begin{bmatrix} 1 & 3 \\ 2 & 4 \end{bmatrix}$
   D) $\begin{bmatrix} 0 & 1 \\ 2 & 4 \end{bmatrix}$
   E) $\begin{bmatrix} 4 & 9 \\ 2 & 4 \end{bmatrix}$

4. The graph of $\frac{x^2}{3} + \frac{y^2}{4} = 1$ is:

   A) a circle
   B) a hyperbola
   C) a straight line
   D) an ellipse
   E) a parabola

5. If $\begin{bmatrix} 1 & 3 \\ -2 & 4 \end{bmatrix}\begin{bmatrix} x \\ y \end{bmatrix} = \begin{bmatrix} 1 \\ 8 \end{bmatrix}$, then find x + y = ?

   A) −3
   B) −2
   C) −1
   D) 0
   E) 1

Matrix Test 21

6. Which of following is graph of $\frac{x^2}{6} + \frac{y^2}{4} = 1$.

A)

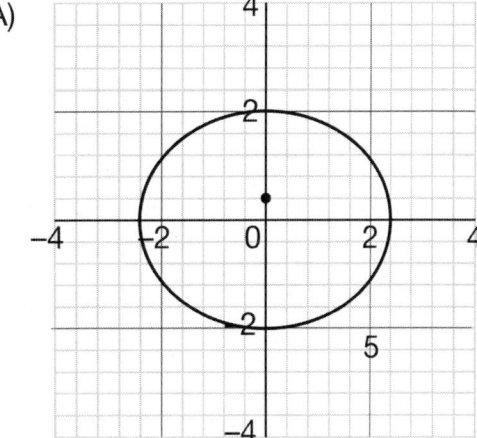

B)

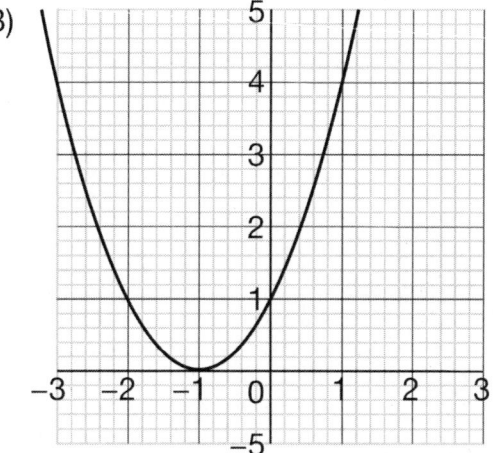

C)

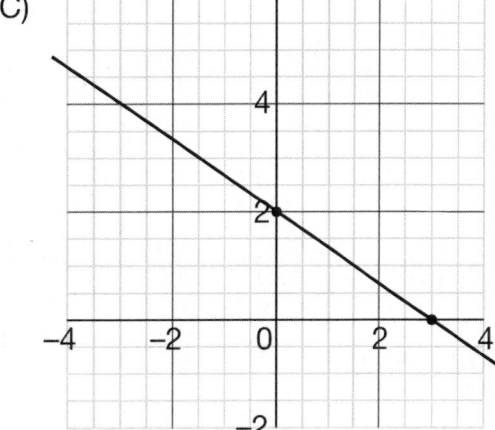

D)

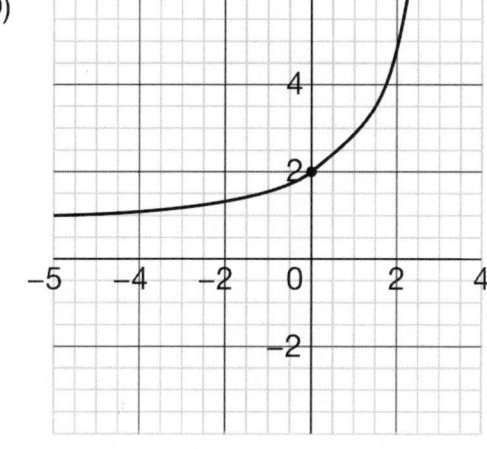

E) None of above

Matrix Test 21

7. $\begin{bmatrix} x & y \\ 2 & 4 \end{bmatrix} = 10$

In the equation above what is the x in terms of y?

A) $\dfrac{y+5}{2}$

B) $\dfrac{y-5}{2}$

C) $\dfrac{y+5}{5}$

D) $\dfrac{y-2}{5}$

E) $\dfrac{y-5}{5}$

8. If $A = \begin{bmatrix} a & b \\ b & d \end{bmatrix}$ and $B = \begin{bmatrix} e & f \\ g & h \end{bmatrix}$, then which of following is A + B?

A) $\begin{bmatrix} a & b \\ c & d \end{bmatrix}$

B) $\begin{bmatrix} e & f \\ g & h \end{bmatrix}$

C) $\begin{bmatrix} a & f \\ b & h \end{bmatrix}$

D) $\begin{bmatrix} a+e, b+f \\ c+g, d+h \end{bmatrix}$

E) $\begin{bmatrix} a-e, b-f \\ c-g, d-h \end{bmatrix}$

9. Which of following is shown the 2×2 identity matrix?

A) $\begin{bmatrix} 0 & 0 \\ 0 & 0 \end{bmatrix}$

B) $\begin{bmatrix} 1 & 1 \\ 0 & 0 \end{bmatrix}$

C) $\begin{bmatrix} 1 & 0 \\ 1 & 0 \end{bmatrix}$

D) $\begin{bmatrix} 0 & 0 \\ 1 & 1 \end{bmatrix}$

E) $\begin{bmatrix} 1 & 0 \\ 0 & 1 \end{bmatrix}$

10. M is a 3×4 matrix, and N is a 4×5 matrix. What are the dimensions of MN?

A) 3×4

B) 3×5

C) 4×5

D) 4×3

E) 3×6

Matrix Test 21
Answer Key

1)	A
2)	E
3)	A
4)	B
5)	C
6)	A
7)	A
8)	D
9)	E
10)	B

Matrix Test 21
Solutions

1. $K \cdot L = [2 \ 4] \cdot \begin{bmatrix} -3 & 4 \\ 2 & -1 \end{bmatrix}$

    $= [2 \cdot (-3) + 4 \cdot 2 \ , \ 2 \cdot 4 + 4 \cdot (-1)]$

    $= [2, 4]$

    Correct Answer : A

2. Divide both sides by 3:

    $\begin{bmatrix} x \\ y \end{bmatrix} = \frac{4}{3} \begin{bmatrix} x & y \\ 2 & 4 \end{bmatrix} \Rightarrow$ Multiply the scalar by each component

    $\begin{bmatrix} x \\ y \end{bmatrix} = \begin{bmatrix} 12 \cdot \frac{4}{3} \\ 18 \cdot \frac{4}{3} \end{bmatrix} \Rightarrow \begin{bmatrix} x \\ y \end{bmatrix} = \begin{bmatrix} 16 \\ 24 \end{bmatrix}$, then x = 16

    and y = 24

    x + y = 16 + 24 = 40

    Correct Answer : E

3. $X = Y + \begin{bmatrix} 1 & 3 \\ 2 & 4 \end{bmatrix} \Rightarrow X = \begin{bmatrix} 3 & 6 \\ 4 & 7 \end{bmatrix} + \begin{bmatrix} 1 & 3 \\ 2 & 4 \end{bmatrix} = \begin{bmatrix} 4 & 9 \\ 6 & 11 \end{bmatrix}$

    Correct Answer : A

4. Hyperbola equation: $\frac{x^2}{a^2} + \frac{y^2}{b^2} = 1$

    Correct Answer : B

5. $\begin{bmatrix} 1 & 3 \\ -2 & 4 \end{bmatrix} \begin{bmatrix} x \\ y \end{bmatrix} = \begin{bmatrix} 1 \cdot x + 3 \cdot y \\ -2 \cdot x + 4 \cdot y \end{bmatrix}$

    $\begin{bmatrix} x + 3y \\ -2x + 4y \end{bmatrix} = \begin{bmatrix} 1 \\ 8 \end{bmatrix} \Rightarrow$

    x + 3y = 1 (multiply by 2 all equation)
    –2x + 4y = 8
    _____
    2x + 6y = 2
    + –2x + 4y = 8
    _____
    10y = 10, y = 1 and x = -2

    x + y = -2 + 1 = -1

    Correct Answer : C

6. Hyperbola equation: $\frac{x^2}{a^2} + \frac{y^2}{b^2} = 1$

    Correct Answer : A

7. $\begin{vmatrix} x & y \\ 2 & 4 \end{vmatrix} = 10 \Rightarrow 4x - 2y = 10$

    4x - 2y = 10

    4x = 2y + 10

    $x = \frac{2y + 10}{4} \Rightarrow x = \frac{y+5}{2}$

    Correct Answer : A

8. $A + B = \begin{bmatrix} a & b \\ c & d \end{bmatrix} + \begin{bmatrix} e & f \\ g & h \end{bmatrix} = \begin{bmatrix} a+e, b+f \\ c+g, d+h \end{bmatrix}$

    Correct Answer : D

9. Identity matrix;

    $\begin{bmatrix} 1 & 0 \\ 0 & 1 \end{bmatrix}$

    Correct Answer : E

10. If M is a 3×4 matrix, and N is a 4×5 matrix, then the dimensions of MN = 3×5

    Correct Answer : B

Mixed Review Test V

1. If $\cos x + \sin x = \sqrt{5} + 1$, then find $\cos x \cdot \sin x = ?$

A) $\dfrac{5 - 2\sqrt{5}}{2}$

B) $\dfrac{5 + 2\sqrt{5}}{2}$

C) $5 - \sqrt{5}$

D) $2 + \sqrt{5}$

E) $2 - \sqrt{5}$

2. If $A = \begin{bmatrix} a & b \\ c & d \end{bmatrix}$ and $B = \begin{bmatrix} e & f \\ g & h \end{bmatrix}$, then which of following is $A - B$?

A) $\begin{bmatrix} a & b \\ c & d \end{bmatrix}$

B) $\begin{bmatrix} e & f \\ g & h \end{bmatrix}$

C) $\begin{bmatrix} a & f \\ b & h \end{bmatrix}$

D) $\begin{bmatrix} a+e, b+f \\ c+g, d+h \end{bmatrix}$

E) $\begin{bmatrix} a-e, b-f \\ c-g, d-h \end{bmatrix}$

3. If $x^3 = y$, then find $\log_y x^2$?

A) 1

B) 2

C) $\dfrac{1}{3}$

D) $\dfrac{2}{3}$

E) $\dfrac{1}{2}$

4. $\begin{bmatrix} a & 6 \\ b & 4 \end{bmatrix} = 18$

In the equation above what is the a in terms of b?

A) $\dfrac{9 + 3b}{2}$

B) $\dfrac{9 + 2b}{3}$

C) $\dfrac{2 + 3b}{9}$

D) $\dfrac{2 + 9b}{3}$

E) $\dfrac{9 - 3b}{2}$

5. In the following figure P is the center of circle, find the area of the shaded region.

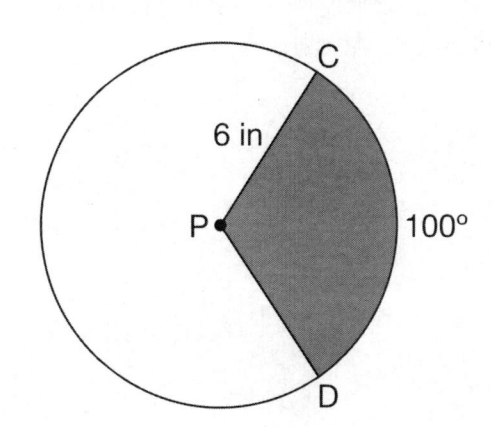

A) 5π

B) 10π

C) 20π

D) 30π

E) 35π

168

Mixed Review Test V

6. $\dfrac{a^{2m}}{a^{10}} = a^6$ and $a^{3n} = a^{30}$, then $m \cdot n$?

   A) 50

   B) 60

   C) 70

   D) 80

   E) 90

7. $\dfrac{1}{3}(6x - 9) + (x - 12) = ax + x + b$

   What is the value of $a - b$?

   A) 6

   B) 9

   C) 12

   D) 17

   E) 19

8. Which of the following is equivalent to the expression below?

   $(x^2y - 2x^2 + 6xy) - (xy^2 - 2x^2 + 4xy)$

   A) $x^2y - xy^2 + 2xy$

   B) $x^2y - xy^2 - 2xy$

   C) $x^2y + xy^2 + 2xy$

   D) $-x^2y - xy^2 - 2xy$

   E) $xy^2 - 2xy - 2y$

9. If $\dfrac{3}{4}x - \dfrac{1}{8}x = \dfrac{1}{12} + \dfrac{2}{3}$, what the value of x?

   A) 6

   B) 7

   C) $\dfrac{6}{7}$

   D) $\dfrac{6}{5}$

   E) 8

10. Which of the following is equivalent to the complex number $\dfrac{3+i}{2-i}$?

    A) $1 - i$

    B) 1

    C) i

    D) $1 + i$

    E) $i - 1$

Mixed Review Test V
Answer Key

1)	B
2)	E
3)	D
4)	A
5)	B
6)	D
7)	D
8)	A
9)	D
10)	D

Mixed Review Test V
Solutions

1. $(\cos x + \sin x)^2 = (\sqrt{5}+1)^2$

$\to \cos^2 x + 2\cos x \cdot \sin x + \sin^2 x = 5 + 2\sqrt{5} + 1$

$\to \cos^2 x + \sin^2 x = 1 \Rightarrow$

$1 + 2\cos x \cdot \sin x = 6 + 2\sqrt{5}$, then

$\sin x \cdot \cos x = \dfrac{5 + 2\sqrt{5}}{2}$

Correct Answer : B

2. $A - B = \begin{bmatrix} a & b \\ c & d \end{bmatrix} - \begin{bmatrix} e & f \\ g & h \end{bmatrix} = \begin{bmatrix} a-e & b-f \\ c-g & d-h \end{bmatrix}$

Correct Answer : E

3. If $x^3 = y \Rightarrow \log_y x^2 = \log_{x^3} x^2 = \dfrac{2}{3}$, $\log_{x^x} = \dfrac{2}{3}$

Correct Answer : D

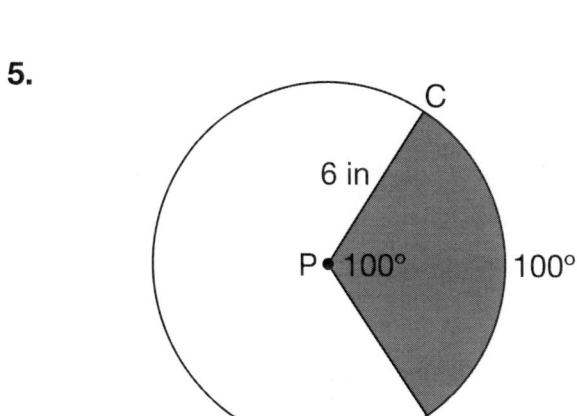

4. $\begin{bmatrix} a & 6 \\ b & 4 \end{bmatrix} = 18 \Rightarrow 4a - 6b = 18$

$4a - 6b = 18$ (divided each term by 2)

$2a - 3b = 9$

$a = \dfrac{9 + 3b}{2}$

Correct Answer : A

5.

Shaded Area $= \dfrac{\pi r^2 \alpha}{360°}$

$= \dfrac{\pi \cdot 6^2 \cdot 100°}{360°}$

$= \dfrac{36\pi \cdot 100°}{360°}$

$= 10\pi$

Correct Answer : B

171

Mixed Review Test V
Solutions

6. $\dfrac{a^{2m}}{a^{10}} = a^6$

$a^{2m-10} = a^6$

$2m - 10 = 6$, $2m = 16$

$m = 8$

$a^{3n} = a^{30}$, $3n = 30$ $n = 10$

$m \cdot n = 8 \cdot 10 = 80$

Correct Answer : D

7. $\dfrac{1}{3}(6x - 9) + (x - 12) = ax + x + b$

$2x - 3 + x - 12 = ax + x + b$

$3x - 15 = x(a + 1) + b$

$b = -15$

$3x = x(a + 1) \Rightarrow a + 1 = 3$, $a = 2$

$a - b = 2 - (-15)$

$= 17$

Correct Answer : D

8. $(x^2y - 2x^2 + 6xy) - (xy^2 - 2x^2 + 4xy)$

$= x^2y - 2x^2 + 6xy - xy^2 + 2x^2 - 4xy$

$x^2y - xy^2 + 2xy$

Correct Answer : A

9. $\dfrac{2 \cdot 3}{2 \cdot 4}x - \dfrac{1}{8}x = \dfrac{1}{12} + \dfrac{2}{3}$

$\dfrac{6x - x}{8} = \dfrac{9}{12}$

$\dfrac{5x}{8} = \dfrac{3}{4}$ $x = \dfrac{6}{5}$

Correct Answer : D

10. $i^2 = -1$

$\dfrac{3+i}{2-i}$

$= \left(\dfrac{3+i}{2-i}\right)\left(\dfrac{2+i}{2+i}\right)$

$= \dfrac{6 + 3i + 2i + i^2}{4 - i^2}$

$= \dfrac{6 + 5i - 1}{4 + 1}$

$= \dfrac{5 + 5i}{5} = 1 + i$

Correct Answer : D

Made in United States
North Haven, CT
05 November 2024